TEACHING INFORMATION LITERACY

A Conceptual Approach

Christy Gavin

The Scarecrow Press, Inc.
Lanham, Maryland • Toronto • Plymouth, UK
2008

SCARECROW PRESS, INC.

Published in the United States of America
by Scarecrow Press, Inc.
A wholly owned subsidiary of
The Rowman & Littlefield Publishing Group, Inc.
4501 Forbes Boulevard, Suite 200, Lanham, Maryland 20706
www.scarecrowpress.com

Estover Road
Plymouth PL6 7PY
United Kingdom

British Library Cataloguing in Publication Information Available

Library of Congress Cataloging-in-Publication Data

Gavin, Christy, 1952–
    Teaching information literacy : a conceptual approach / Christy Gavin.
        p. cm.
    Includes bibliographical references and index.
    ISBN-13: 978-0-8108-5202-0 (pbk. : alk. paper)
    ISBN-10: 0-8108-5202-0 (pbk. : alk. paper)
    1. Information literacy–Study and teaching (Higher) 2. Research–
Methodology–Study and teaching (Higher) 3. Library orientation for college
students. 4. Electronic information resource literacy–Study and teaching
(Higher) 5. Internet research–Study and teaching (Higher) 6. Internet
searching–Study and teaching (Higher) I. Title.
ZA3075.G38 2008
028.7071'1–dc22   2007017222

CONTENTS

FIGURES AND TABLES

FIGURES

TABLES

INTRODUCTION:
INFORMATION VS. WISDOM

> Where is the wisdom we've lost in knowledge? Where is the knowledge we've lost in information?[1]

Today, many incoming college freshmen consider themselves information savvy because they feel they are very familiar with the hardware and software of information technology, such as the Web, e-mail, and cell phones. Their seeming familiarity with the Web leads students to be overly confident of their research skills, often minimizing the research process by assuming that gathering facts is the endgame of the research process. But, of course, rigorous research practices demand a much more intellectual workout. Novice students must leave the pedagogical comfort zone of high school where they learned bits of knowledge fed to them incrementally by their teachers. They must set aside prescribed ways of learning and pursue truth by way of systematic, independent inquiry. And pursuing truth systematically requires researchers to be skilled in information competencies to prepare them to ask relevant questions, search resources with sophistication, derive meaning from information, and make informed decisions based on the knowledge they have acquired. In other words, individuals who are open to free inquiry progress through four stages of knowledge: data, information, knowledge, and wisdom. As David Moursund observes, "Data can be collected and stored. Computers can transform raw data into information. Through study and thinking, people transform information into personal knowledge. People gain wisdom by integrating and analyzing their accumulated knowledge."[2] Ideally, then, students trained in the basic information competencies know that there is more to research than just popping keywords into a search engine, gathering a bunch of facts, and restating them in a required assignment. Underlying information competencies—that is, conducting research from a conceptual approach—better prepares students to:

- recognize the research need or problem;
- formulate questions to search for ideas, answers, and solutions;
- mine the relevant resources to retrieve the most relevant information;
- convert relevant information to knowledge by analyzing it, reflecting upon it, and evaluating it; and
- integrate the knowledge so that they can make informed decisions and sound judgments.

By intellectually moving through each of these stages, students will be able to distinguish between data, information, knowledge, and wisdom. In becoming more prudent and discerning researchers, they will realize that amassing information is a mindless activity unless one knows what do with it. Success depends upon using critical reasoning skills and imagination to investigate a research question, develop a thesis, access relevant sources; evaluate the validity of these resources, and provide cogent arguments and conclusions. As students progress through the research experience, they will become more confident in:

- extending their creative powers,
- learning to make relationships between ideas,
- transferring ideas to other contexts,
- integrating what is known with personal experiences, and
- studying the opinions of the "other," that is, suspending their preconceived notions and thinking open-mindedly when considering issues or solving a problem.

INFORMATION LITERACY BEYOND THE CLASSROOM

Students will be called upon to use and refine their information-seeking skills to make informed decisions in real life, especially the workplace. Increasingly, business organizations realize that to be competitive, they must sustain an "information edge" by expertly managing their intellectual capital. That is, to turn a profit, a company must exploit its intangible human assets—knowledge, skills, and experience. Gone are the days of the attitude "Smart's nice, but I like money."[3] Rather, business organizations see themselves as "learning organizations" that acknowledge that to fulfill their strategic mission, their employees must be skilled in information retrieval, information analysis, and application of knowledge and experiences gained from analysis. As Tom W. Goad observes in his book *Information Literacy and Workplace Performance*, "the organizations that will be [successful] will be the ones that help their people excel at being information literate—having information power."[4]

LIBRARIANS' UNIQUE ROLE

In this so-called information age, students, like the public, often mistake data and information for knowledge and, if they consider it at all, misinterpret knowledge for wisdom. One reason is that many students, like their elders, are seduced by the power of Web technology to deliver information easily and conveniently. They believe that the Web can provide all the answers they need to satisfy their academic needs. As Rita Vine, an information professional, remarks, "To most users the world is just a giant bunch of information behind a screen, all of it accessible by keyword."[5]

Librarians, of course, know that this assumption is wrongheaded. They also know that they are essential in the process of students becoming astute information seekers and thinkers. However, this may be news to many students. As Gary Price, librarian and coauthor of *The Invisible Web*, observes, "librarians still have an image problem in an age when the professional information gatherer's services should be more valuable than ever."[6] Price's observation is born out by Internet usage studies that show that students do not initially turn to a librarian for research assistance.[7] Moreover, as librarians know from experience, and which several studies support, library instruction can influence how students perceive research sources and persuade students to recognize the value of an array of research tools other than Google.[8]

Librarians' power in persuasion lies in their perspective and training; they view knowledge globally, understand how information is disseminated, know the complexities of search tools, and thus can find highly relevant material quickly and efficiently. Through formal and informal instruction, librarians can convince students that there are content-rich sources beyond the free Web and can help them feel comfortable in using them. Librarians help students learn to become effective information seekers and thinkers by foregrounding process over mechanics, that is, by teaching students to research independently. This involves inculcating and demonstrating the importance of framing cogent questions, developing solid theses, formulating logical search strategies, and evaluating retrieved information. And in so doing, librarians collaborate with faculty in guiding students through the intellectual stages that lead to knowledge and wisdom that will benefit them now and in their future lives.

TEACHING STUDENTS TO BE INDEPENDENT RESEARCHERS

How does one deliver effective instruction to college students who consider learning library research about as exciting as a trip to the supermarket and as painful as a visit to the dentist? The challenge for instructors, experienced as well as those new to the field, is to create and deliver diverse, dynamic instruction that will provide students with the tools and knowledge they need to conduct research for their courses and allow them to carry those skills to the workplace. This book aims to meet that challenge by providing teaching librarians and others who deliver instruction in information literacy fresh approaches to teaching specific concepts, such as developing a topic and thesis, constructing Boolean strategies, and evaluating the credibility of a source.

The primary pedagogical framework for this book is a concept-based approach that teaches students the information-seeking strategies and critical-thinking abilities needed to do effective research. Crucial to this approach is the emphasis on thinking skills, which include basic skills (observing, comparing, contrasting, and classifying) and more complex skills (analysis, logical reasoning, problem solving, and evaluating). Chapters are arranged sequentially to simulate a typical research process. Thus, chapters 1 and 2 discuss preparing a research topic and thesis, while chapters 4 through focus on the search strategies and content evaluation for three major research tools: online book catalogs, periodical databases, and Internet search engines. Chapter 3 focuses on Boolean search methodology that can be applied to each of these research tools.

Within each chapter, a set of learning objectives is discussed, followed by class activities, instructor guides, and assessment tools developed by the author and other instructors. The chapters are designed to help instructors in three ways. First, instructors can draw from the content to create a particular component. Second, instructors can adapt pertinent content to deepen and enliven lectures and discussions, thus avoiding banal and superficial presentations. Third, the content, guides, and activities can assist in developing custom assessment instruments.

NOTES

1. T. S. Eliot, "Choruses from the 'The Rock,'" in *Selected Poems* (New York: Harcourt, Brace and World, 1936), 107.

2. David Moursund, "Data, Information, Knowledge, Wisdom," *Learning and Leading with Technology* 26 (1999): 4–5.

3. Thomas Stewart, "Intellectual Capital: Ten Years Later, How Far We've Come," *Fortune*, May 2001, 192.

4. Tom W. Goad, *Information Literacy and Workplace Performance* (Westport, CT: Quorum, 2002), 15.

5. Sue Bowness, "Librarians vs. Technology: Expertise in an Age of Amateur Researchers," *Information Highways*, November/December 2004, www.econtentinstitute.org/issues/table_of_contents.asp. Vine's comment seems to be supported by recent surveys on Internet usage. The *Pew Internet and American Life Project* (2004, www.pewinternet.org) revealed that 84 percent of American adults use a search engine to find information on the Internet. Moreover, according to a 2004 study conducted by USC's Annenberg School of Communications (www.digitalcenter.org), the majority of Internet users consider the Internet as their major source of current information.

6. Bowness, "Librarians vs. Technology."

7. Studies that show that students turn to the Internet first rather than to a librarian include: Steve Jones, "Internet Goes to College: How Students Are Living in the Future with Today's Technology," *Pew Internet and American Life Project*, September 15, 2002, www.pewinternet.org/pdfs/PIP_College_Report. pdf; OCLC, "White Paper on the Information Habits of College Students: How Academic Librarians Can Influence Students' Web-Based Information Choices," June 2002; Deborah J. Grimes and Carl H. Boening, "Worries with the Web: A Look at Student Use of Web Resources," *College & Research Libraries* 62 (January 2001): 11–23; Shippensburg University, Ezra Lehman Memorial Library, "Internet Use Survey—Analysis," September 26, 2000, www. ship.edu/~bhl/survey; Bradley P. Tolppanen, "A Survey of World Wide Web Use by Freshman English Students: Results and Implications for Bibliographic Instruction," *Internet Reference Services Quarterly* 4 (1999): 43–53; John Lubans, "How First-Year Students Use and Regard Internet Resources," 1998, www.lubans.org/docs/1styear/firstyear.html.

8. For a recent study on the influence of library instruction on student attitudes toward research, see Shawn V. Lombardo and Cynthia E. Miree, "Caught in the Web: The Impact of Library Instruction on Business Students' Perceptions and Use of Print and Online Sources," *College and Research Libraries* 64, no.1 (January 2003): 6–22. The authors also provide an overview of past research on the influence of library instruction on student attitudes toward information resources.

1

SELECTING AND NARROWING TOPICS

Basic research is what I do when I don't know what I am doing.[1]

> Goal: To formulate a viable topic.
> Objective 1: Select a topic.
> Objective 2: Narrow a topic.

Selecting a subject stymies most undergraduates. Why? They often approach a subject at a distinct disadvantage: they know virtually little or nothing about the subject area they are to research. If asked, most students can write a short essay on their favorite hobbies in twenty minutes, yet few of those same students can write five paragraphs on the theory of relativity. Writing about what is familiar is much easier than writing about what is alien. Therefore, students must begin the topic development process by discovering what has been said by others about a subject.

LEARNING OBJECTIVES AND INSTRUCTOR ACTIVITIES

Objective 1: Select a Topic.

A plethora of media offers students an endless supply of possible subjects to study. Many of these sources can also provide a deep background of a subject. Most are jargon-free and can increase students' stores of knowledge while affording them a jumping-off place for ideas from which to develop a research question. Encourage students to browse the following:

- textbooks
- specialized encyclopedias
- popular or trade magazines
- library and bookstore shelves
- Web directories (e.g., Google)
- tables of contents of key journals

For students who explore the pros and cons of an issue, point them toward sources that bring together arguments representing the various sides of an issue. The following sources provide topics and background material for controversial subjects:

- Taking Sides series (McGraw Hill/Dushkin) (www.dushkin.com/takingsides)
- Opposing Viewpoints series (Greenhaven Press) (www.wadsworth.com/pubco/serv_opposing.html)

Nontraditional media can also be a source of research topics. These may include TV and radio talk shows, news programs, and even movies. For example, the film *A Beautiful Mind* could inspire a student to explore the destigmatization of schizophrenia.

Objective 2: Narrow a Topic.

Scenario:

CRIMINOLOGY STUDENT: Okay, I got a subject, "crimes in America." Now what do I do?
  INSTRUCTOR: Read and question.
  CRIMINOLOGY STUDENT: Huh?

Once a topic has been chosen, the tendency of novice researchers is to use Google to retrieve the required number of sources and string them together to obtain the requisite number of pages. They turn in papers with the belief that they have done research, yet they are astonished to learn that their poor grades are due to lack of cohesiveness and weak research. Contrary to what many students believe, research is not simply "looking up stuff," but rather a systematic inquiry into a distinct aspect of a topic. To initiate a systematic inquiry, students must conduct preliminary research by finding a few sources on a topic, skimming the material, selecting what is useful, and then reading it closely. This way, students gain a working knowledge of the topic and are in a much better position to determine what research approaches are worth investigating.

Narrowing a topic works best if three basic investigative tools (heuristics) are used:

1. Brainstorming: helps to break down subject.
2. Clustering and classifying: helps to organize ideas generated by brainstorming.
3. Asking questions: initiates an understanding of the subject and exploration of its facets.

The following section shows how these heuristic tools can be used in the topic development process.

1. Brainstorming During the topic-development stage, brainstorming, or free associating, is an excellent way of stimulating creativity. Developed by advertising executive Alex Osborn, brainstorming encourages freewheeling ideas, no matter how wild, mundane, profound, or silly.[2] As more ideas emerge, students build upon them or combine them with other ideas. And because brainstorming discourages tunnel vision and the evaluation of ideas, the tendency to censor topics is less likely to occur.

2. Clustering and Classifying Clustering and classifying are strategies that students use to record information generated by brainstorming. These techniques help students ascertain patterns and connections between known facts and new ideas and concepts.

2a. Clustering Clustering is random and nonlinear and thus appeals to students who are visual or intuitive learners. The following steps outline clustering:

1. Select the subject "crime" and brainstorm subtopics.
2. Select one of the subtopics.
3. Brainstorm the subtopic.
4. Focus on one of the sub-subtopics.
5. Research the sub-subtopic.

Figures 1.1 through 1.3 illustrate the clustering process. Steps 3 and 4 (figure 1.2) involve students reading articles on Internet stock fraud for ideas on how to approach the topic. Thus, step 5 (figure 1.3) in the cluster process might look like this:

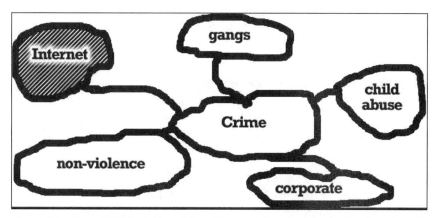

Figure 1.1   Step (1) Select the subject Crime and brainstorm subtopics, Step (2) Choose one of the subtopics

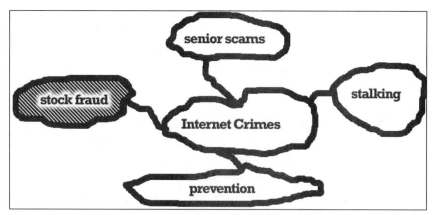

Figure 1.2   Step (3) Brainstorm the subtopic, Step (4) Focus on one of the sub-subtopics

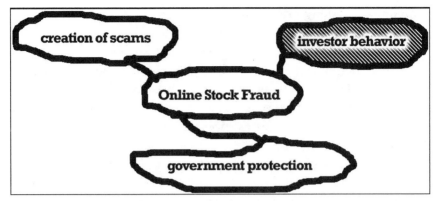

Figure 1.3   Step (5) Focus on online stock fraud and investor behavior

See examples 1.1 through 1.5 for more models of clustering.

2b. Classifying   Unlike clustering, the classification device orders information sequentially, which appeals to linear thinkers who are more comfortable with a systematic approach, beginning with A and working through a sequence until completing Z. For example:

Topic:
Place:
Time period:
Person/group (historical figure, population segment, political entity):
Event or Aspect:
Problem or Issue:

The following example illustrates how the topic "Internet" can be narrowed by classifying it:

Topic: Internet
Place: United States
Time period: last ten years
Person/group: investors
Aspect: online fraud
Problem: protecting investors from online scams

See example 1.6 for more models of classifying.

Objective 3: Asking Questions.

While asking questions of the material should be done at all stages of the term-paper process, it is especially powerful in topic development. Queries, particularly open-ended queries, enable students to explore what is under the surface of a subject in order to discover its hidden terrains. The following discusses specific heuristic guides that can help students begin the query process.

Students can begin their questions by using the traditional reporter query words: Who? What? Where? Why? When? How? For example, a student could explore the topic "online investment scams" by asking:

- Who are the victims of Internet fraud? Who tempts them?
- Why do investors become victims of online scams?
- What kinds of scams occur? What is being done to protect investors? and
- How do these scams work? How do investors avoid them?

If students are examining points of view, they may begin their questions with: if, should, does, will, and can. Or, students beginning to explore scientific topics can begin their queries with the following phrases: "Is there a correlation between . . . ?" or "Is there a relationship between . . . ?"

A variation on the above set of "reporter" questions is rhetorician Kenneth Burke's[3] pentad of key terms—act, scene, agent, agency, and purpose:

Act: What was done? What took place in thought or deed?
Scene: When or where was the act done? What the was background of the act? What was the situation in which it occurred?
Agent: Who did the act? What kind of person[s]?
Agency: How did they do the act? What means or instruments did they use?
Purpose: Why was the act done?

These key terms serve as a way to investigate the motivations of human action. The pentad works very well in researching literary texts.

The following questions were developed by Jacqueline Berke and Randal Woodland:[4]

- How can X be described?
- How did X happen?
- What kind of person is X?
- What is my memory of X?
- What is my personal response to X?
- What are the facts about X?
- What does X mean?
- What is the essential function of X?
- What are the component parts of X?
- How is X made or done?
- What are the causes of X?
- What are the consequences of X?
- What are the types of X?
- How does X compete with Y?
- What is the present status of X?
- How can X be summarized?
- How should X be interpreted?
- What is the value of X?
- What case can be made for or against X?

See examples 1.7 through 1.12 for more models of framing questions.

Asking questions stimulates further thinking about the subject. And, with practice, students will gain query skills that will strengthen their ability to make sense of the material, retain information, and synthesize and evaluate information. Moreover, students will soon learn to use tools of inquiry to critique their own term papers and determine if a particular section is unclear or needs to be fleshed out.

The investigative tools of clustering, classifying, and querying challenge students to look below the surface of a topic in pursuit of truth. The payoff, students soon realize, is that they have gained control over something that they initially perceived as an overwhelming, chaotic jumble of information. As students grasp the big picture and what lies beyond it, their self-confidence increases, motivating them to focus on a particular angle and pursue its intricacies.

The key to success at the topic-development stage is creative inquiry. This particular learning process conflicts with the learning processes students are exposed to in elementary and secondary school where, in the era of standardized testing, information is given to them in bits and pieces, encouraging students to be dependent on teachers as dispensers of information. Yet, success in creative thinking and problem solving depends upon the learner's ability to acquire knowledge independently by searching for answers and finding solutions to problems.

CLASS ACTIVITIES

One-Hour Sessions

1. One-hour sessions do not allow much time for discussion to develop topics, however students will pay attention if library research strategies are linked to the topics that they must address.
2. When introducing key sources in a discipline or subject area, such as special encyclopedias or handbooks, emphasize how these sources can help students narrow their topics. If time permits, select an entry from one of the sources and demonstrate the narrowing process by highlighting subtopics mentioned in the entry.
3. To show the brainstorming process, write a broad topic on the board. Ask the class to cluster ideas. Then, focus on one subtopic and ask them to them develop a research question based on the subtopic. See examples 1.1 through 1.12.

Multiple Sessions and Courses

1. Incorporate strategies mentioned in the previous section on one-hour sessions.
2. If the topic is a controversial social issue, have students brainstorm different perspectives. For example, "school prayer" will be viewed differently by an atheist, a Catholic, a Republican, and a Democrat.
3. Write a broad topic on the board. Have students practice clustering, classifying, and querying by assigning them a broad topic (see examples 1.1 through 1.12). Discuss their results in class. Then, focus on one subtopic (or connect it to another) and develop a rough research

question. Discuss. Follow up by asking students to develop their own topic by using clustering, classifying, and querying.

4. Show how research questions can be converted into a rough thesis statement. See chapter 2 for information on thesis development.

5. While many students tend to tackle a broad topic, others begin too narrowly, such as "teen pregnancy in Smalltown, U.S.A." Short of using local resources, this sort of topic will be very difficult to research. Show how narrowing techniques can also assist in broadening a topic to a manageable size.

6. Ask students to keep a research journal. On a cognitive level, the use of a research journal helps students think through what they are planning, doing, and learning and helps them think about and question the actual process of research. On a practical level, a research journal helps students become more organized and provides a place for dialogue between the librarian, the composition instructor, and the student.[5]

7. Help students understand how topics germinate in the professional realm.

INSTRUCTOR GUIDES, HANDOUTS, AND EXERCISES

1. Examples 1.1–1.5: Clustering examples
2. Example 1.6: Classifying examples
3. Examples 1.7–1.12: Framing questions examples
4. Example 1.13: Topic development exercise

Websites on Topic Development

1. California State University, Bakersfield Library, "Developing a Topic," www.csub.edu/library/infocomp.shtml. Provides explanations and examples on narrowing a topic.

2. LeTourneau University, Owlet Writing and Learning, "Stock Issues in Argument" (2002), owlet.letu.edu/contenthtml/research/stockissues.html stockissues.html. Provides a detailed chart of questions to ask when exploring an issue or solving a problem.

3. Online Library Learning, "Unit Two: Starting Your Research," www.usg.edu/galileo/skills/unit02/index.phtml. Tutorial introduces users to developing topics and choosing appropriate sources.

4. Pennsylvania State University Libraries, "Concept Map" (November 9, 2006), www.libraries.psu.edu/instruction/infolit/andyou/mod1/pre.htm. Exercise on developing topics using the clustering method.

5. Radford University, "Library Tutorial: Research Strategy" (September 14, 2005), lib.radford.edu/Tutorial. Introduces students to developing a topic and creating search statements.

6. State University of New York, Oswego, "Information Literacy Tutorial" (July 12, 2005), www.oswego.edu/library/tutorial. Presents the basics of topic development with examples drawn from *CQ Researcher*. Includes a worksheet.

7. University of Buffalo, "Research Assistant: Choosing a Topic," ublib.buffalo.edu/libraries/asl/tutorials/research.html. Connects explanations of developing a topic with concrete examples.

8. University of Richmond, "Getting Started: Brainstorming," writing2.richmond.edu/writing/wweb/brainst.html. Illustrates brainstorming by developing the topic "ethics of cigarette advertising."

9. University of Texas, Austin, "Substantial Writing Component Resources: Brainstorming" (2002), www.swc.utexas.edu/planning/process.shtml. Discusses a variety of brainstorming techniques.

10. University of Utah, Health Sciences Library, "Internet Navigator: Modules 3," www-navigator.utah.edu. This interactive tutorial includes assignments and quizzes.

11. University of Wyoming Libraries, "TIP: Tutorial for Information Power," tip.uwyo.edu/intro1.htm. Includes an exercise on determining appropriate research questions.

Assessment Tools

1. To reinforce what they have learned, ask students to narrow their own topics by using one or more of the narrowing strategies discussed in this chapter. See examples 1.1 through 1.12.

2. Example 1.13 is an exercise that asks students to cluster, classify, and query a topic of their choice.

APPENDIX: EXAMPLES

Steps One and Two

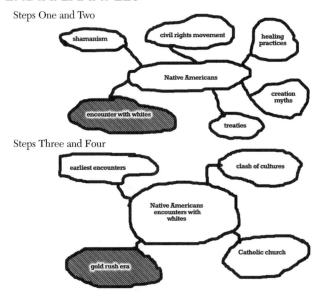

Steps Three and Four

Figure 1.4

Example 1.1: Clustering Example, Native Americans

Steps One and Two

Steps Three and Four

Figure 1.5

Example 1.2: Clustering Example, Religion

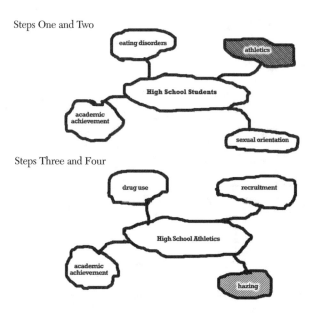

Figure 1.6

Example 1.3: Clustering Example, High School Students

Figure 1.7

Example 1.4: Clustering Example, Toni Morrison's *Beloved*

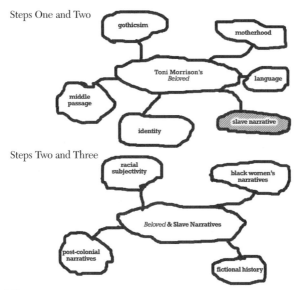

Figure 1.8

Example 1.4: Clustering Example, *Beloved* and Slave Narratives

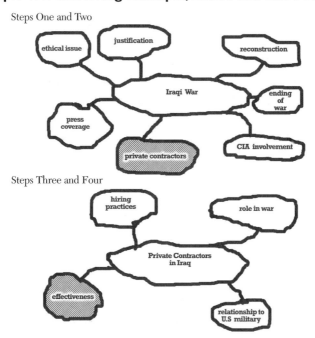

Figure 1.9

Example 1.5: Clustering Example, Iraqi War

Example 1.6: Classifying Examples

1. Topic: American Indians
   Place: California
   Time: nineteenth century
   Event: gold rush
   Problem: How were the cultural life and the environment of
   American Indians disrupted by the influx of gold seekers?
2. Topic: religion
   Place: United States
   Time period: 2001 to present
   Person/group: Bush administration
   Aspect: faith-based initiatives
   Issue: Have faith-based initiatives been effective?
3. Topic: high school students
   Place: United States
   Time period: present
   Person/group: student athletes
   Issue: Why is hazing becoming increasingly violent?
4. Topic: Toni Morrison's *Beloved*
   Person/group: Sethe, Denver, and Beloved
   Problem: How does Sethe define Beloved and Denver as
   daughters?
5. Topic: Toni Morrison's *Beloved*
   Historical group: slaves
   Aspect: slave narratives
   Problem: In what ways does Morrison subvert the traditional slave
   narrative?
6. Topic: Iraqi War
   Person/group: private contractors
   Issue: Are private contractors effective in the reconstruction of
   Iraq?

Example 1.7: Framing Questions, American Indians

1. What impact did the huge population influx during the gold rush
   have on California American Indians?

2. How did American Indians react to whites migrating to California?
3. How did whites perceive the American Indians?
4. Did American Indians mine gold? If so, were they free agents or did they work for whites?
5. How did the white miners treat American Indian miners? Were there tensions in the gold fields?
6. Why did the government pass laws that discriminated against American Indians?
7. In what ways were the cultural life and the environment of American Indians disrupted by the influx of gold seekers?
8. Was gold valued by American Indians before the appearance of whites?

Example 1.8: Framing Questions, Faith-Based Initiatives

1. Why did President Bush open federal funding to religious organizations?
2. Does federal funding undermine separation of church and state?
3. Since their inception in 2001, have faith-based initiatives been effective?
4. Do all religions qualify for funding?
5. Have religious organizations received federal funding prior to the faith-based initiatives?
6. Will federal funding be available for programs run by the Nation of Islam?

Example 1.9: Framing Questions, High School Hazing

1. Who participates in high school hazing?
2. What is hazing?
3. What is the purpose of hazing rituals? Are they useful in teaching pledges certain values?
4. If so, what values?
5. What can coaches and administrators do to reduce hazing crimes?
6. What is being done to stop hazing-related violence?

7. How does the sport culture foster hazing?
8. Why do students participate in hazing?
9. Why is hazing becoming increasingly violent?
10. Should hazing be banned?
11. Should prosecutors file charges against violent hazers?
12. If so, what are some healthy alternatives that can replace students' unfulfilled needs that hazing satisfies?
13. Is there a correlation between poor self-esteem and hazing?

Example 1.10: Framing Questions, Toni Morrison's *Beloved* and Motherhood

1. How does Sethe see herself?
2. What kind of mother is she?
3. Why did Sethe kill her baby?
4. What circumstances drove Sethe to kill her baby?
5. What were the consequences of her act?
6. When did Sethe realize that Beloved was her dead child?
7. Does Denver love her mother? If so, how does she love her?
8. What relationship did Sethe have with her mother?
9. Does Beloved have more than one "mother"?
10. How do Beloved and Denver define Sethe as a mother?
11. How does Sethe define Beloved and Denver as daughters?

Example 1.11: Framing Questions, Toni Morrison's *Beloved* and Slave Narratives

1. What is a slave narrative?
2. Why were slave narratives published? What was their purpose?
3. How do the narratives of slave women differ from those of their male counterparts?
4. Are there similarities and differences between *Beloved* and traditional slave narratives?
5. How does *Beloved* fit in the tradition of neo–slave narratives?
6. Does *Beloved* subvert the traditional forms of the slave narrative?

7. Why did Morrison use the slave narrative as a writing strategy?

Example 1.12: Framing Questions, Private Contractors in Iraq

1. What is the role of private contractors working on U.S.-funded projects in Iraq?
2. What are the benefits of relying on the private sector for support services and operations?
3. What major projects have been completed by private contractors in Iraq?
4. How effective are private contractors in completing government contracts?
5. Have private contractors been involved in illegal actions?

Example 1.13: Topic Development, Exercise

Choose a topic related to your research project. To help you narrow the topic, use the methods discussed in class: clustering, classifying, and questioning.

1. Identify your general topic.
2. Narrow the topic by using these methods:
   A. Clustering
   B. Classifying:
   Place:
   Time:
   Person/group:
   Event or aspect:
   Problem or issue:
   C. Questioning
   Explore your topic further by writing four questions concerning your topic. Your questions should be specific. For example, the question "Is animal experimentation good?" is vague. Rephrase for a more thought-provoking question, such as "How reliable is animal-based research?"

List at least two sources that you have used that have helped you better understand your topic. Include: title of source, author of source, and date.

NOTES

1. Wernher von Braun, German American rocket scientist.

2. Alex Osborn, *Applied Imagination: Principles and Procedures for Creative Problem Solving.* (New York: Scribner, 1961).

3. Kenneth Burke, *A Grammar of Motives.* (New York: Prentice Hall, 1945.), xv.

4. Jacqueline Berke and Randal Woodland. *Twenty Questions for the Writer: A Rhetoric with Readings.* (Fort Worth: Harcourt Brace, 1995), 89–90. Refer to their text for further discussion and examples.

5. For additional information on research journals, see Trixie G. Smith, "Keeping Track: Librarians and Composition Instructors, and Student Writers Use the Research Journal," *Research Strategies* 18 (2001): 21–28.

②

DEVELOPING
A THESIS STATEMENT

CONTROVERSY, n. A battle in which spittle or ink replaces the injurious cannon-ball and the inconsiderate bayonet.[1]

Goal: To know and develop a thesis statement.
Objective 1: Identify an argumentative thesis.
Objective 2: Identify a descriptive or informative thesis.

Scenario:

INSTRUCTOR: What exactly is a thesis statement?
STUDENT A: It's the topic of your paper.
STUDENT B: It's what you want to talk about.
STUDENT C: It's the central point.

Students who give responses such as these have a vague if imprecise notion of what a thesis is. They know that it is pivotal to the term paper, but they are fuzzy as to exactly what makes the thesis the "central point." Clearly, what many students fail to realize is that, yes, the thesis is the central idea, but it must be *controlled* by a particular claim, position, stance, point of view, or argument. This is why topic development is difficult for many students: it's one thing to discuss a particular topic but quite another to formulate an acceptable argument from the general topic that can be supported by outside evidence. But finding suitable arguments—intellectual clashes, skirmishes, and debates—is easier if students are willing to learn the whys and wherefores of their chosen topics: the issues, concepts, competing theories, trends, or historical contexts. Reading about a topic's intellectual landscape enables a researcher to become familiar with those areas that engender controversy and debate among experts, scholars, intellectuals, and journalists.

LEARNING OBJECTIVES AND INSTRUCTOR ACTIVITIES

Objective 1: Identify an Argumentative Thesis.

When writers develop an argumentative thesis, they assume that, while not everyone may agree with the assertion, they hope they can persuade readers to see the truth as they see it. An assertion defines a writer's position on an issue, proposes a solution to a problem, or defends a theoretical approach. However, when writers address a topic, they are not allowed the luxury of straddling the proverbial fence. In addition, to ensure clarity and focus, thesis statements should be written in one sentence or, if the assertion is complex, two to three sentences. Here are some examples of argumentative theses:

- Feminism has been beneficial to women, or Feminism has not been beneficial to women.
- The death penalty should be abolished, or The death penalty should not be abolished.
- The mass extinction of the dinosaurs was caused by a huge asteroid colliding with the earth, or Dinosaurs disappeared from the planet due to a series of violent volcanic eruptions that released poisonous gases into the atmosphere.

Whether formulated in one sentence or three, the thesis must contain two parts—a topic and an assertion (or stance, position, opinion, point of view, solution, etc.). The second part of the thesis proves the greatest challenge to students. Often they claim what is obvious to most people or state facts that remain unchallenged:

- Each year guns kill lots of people.
- Smoking is an unhealthy habit.
- Dr. Martin Luther King Jr. is an important figure in African American history.

Granted, the previous statements beg the question "So what?" but they can provide the student a starting point from which to develop a significant argument. For example, the lackluster statement "Lots of people are killed from guns" serves as a catalyst for the more provocative thesis: "Gun control reduces the crime rate." The former statement fails to challenge conventional thinking, while the second argues for a solution that is very controversial.

Objective 2: Identify a Descriptive or Informative Thesis.

Unlike the argumentative thesis, the descriptive thesis allows writers to straddle the fence and to remain neutral without having to commit to a particular side of an issue, solution, or theory. A descriptive thesis does not advocate; it gives an account of something; it explains concepts, characteristics, or features; or it clarifies the various arguments of issues or facets of problems. Here are some examples of descriptive theses:

- During the 1960s, feminism was an important movement.
- Since its resumption in the 1970s, the death penalty has been a very controversial issue among Americans.
- There are three major theories as to why dinosaurs became extinct.

Because descriptive theses simply describe or inform, they lack the tension of persuading the reader to a particular truth. This may be the reason why college-level instructors find descriptive theses unacceptable, agreeing with William Hazlitt who says: "When a thing ceases to be a subject of controversy, it ceases to be a subject of interest."[2]

There is no simple way to teach students how to recognize or write a thesis. Its success depends upon students' willingness to familiarize themselves with a topic's intellectual landscape so that they are knowledgeable enough to write a thesis, unencumbered by absurd or flawed conclusions, faulty logic, or erroneous evidence. Once students develop a working thesis, 50 percent of the work involved in developing the term paper is completed because the remainder of the work will focus solely on gathering, synthesizing, and organizing data that supports the thesis.

CLASS ACTIVITIES

One-Hour Sessions

At the beginning of the session, write a thesis that relates to the students' course subject; it serves as a reference point for the library research strategies that will be taught. For examples and templates, see examples 2.1 through 2.3. Refer to the thesis when discussing discipline-specific research resources.

Multiple Sessions and Courses

1. As an in-class assignment, have students narrow a topic by using one or more of the narrowing techniques in chapter 1. Ask them to develop a question stemming from the narrowed topic. Then, have them "answer" the question by formulating a thesis statement.
2. Give students a list of problematic theses and ask them to critique each one individually or in small groups. Discuss each thesis, and then ask them to try to improve the thesis.
3. Good theses answer well-written questions. Have students write a series of questions based on a subtopic, select one of the questions, and develop a rough thesis.
4. Write a topic on the board and ask the students to develop an argumentative thesis and a descriptive thesis. Write some of the results on the board and discuss.
5. Ask students to evaluate thesis statements. See the exercise and instructor's discussion guide in examples 2.4 and 2.5.

INSTRUCTOR GUIDES, HANDOUTS, AND EXERCISES

1. Example 2.1: Sample Thesis Statements
2. Example 2.2: Argumentative Theses, Templates
3. Example 2.3: Descriptive Theses, Templates
4. Examples 2.4–2.5: Thesis Statement, Exercise and Instructor's Guide

Websites on Thesis Development

1. California State University, Bakersfield Library. "Developing a Thesis Statement" (August 26, 2004), www.lib.csub.edu/info-comp/infocomp.html. Provides explanations and examples on narrowing a topic.
2. Dartmouth College, "Developing Your Thesis," *Writing at Dartmouth* (October 18, 2004), www.dartmouth.edu/~writing/resources/student/ac_paper/develop.shtml. Provides a checklist of what makes a good thesis.
3. Indiana University, Herman B. Wells Library, "Writing Book Reviews" (July 6, 2004), www.indiana.edu/~wts/pamphlets.shtml. Discusses the strengths and weaknesses of thesis statements; includes examples.
4. Northern Michigan University Department of English, "Thesis or Question" (September 13, 2006), www-instruct.nmu.edu/english/WritingCenter. Discusses the differences between thesis statements and research questions.
5. Purdue University, "OWL Online Writing Lab: Writing a Thesis Statement" (2002), owl.english.purdue.edu/handouts/general/gl_thesis.html. Discusses three types of thesis statements: argumentative, explanatory, and analytical.
6. Queen's University, "Developing a Thesis Statement," *The Writing Centre* (April 14, 2005), library.queensu.ca/libguides/guides_theses.htm. Suggests that students can develop a thesis by organizing their thoughts around a Who/How/Why strategy; chart included.
7. Richard H. Robbins, "Thesis Statements," *Global Problems and the Culture of Capitalism* (September 12, 1998), faculty.plattsburgh.edu/richard.robbins/legacy/thesis_statements.html. Robbins's site provides course materials to support his book,

published by Allyn and Bacon, on global issues. Included are fifty-eight thesis statements on international issues: consumerism, labor, hunger, population, health, and race relations.

8. University of Buffalo, "Research Assistant: Choosing a Topic" (2004), ublib.buffalo.edu/libraries/asl/tutorials/research.html. Connects explanations of developing topics with concrete examples.

9. University of North Carolina, Chapel Hill, Writing Center, "Thesis Statements" (2005), www.unc.edu/depts/wcweb/handouts/thesis.html. Provides several examples of strong and weak theses.

10. University of Toronto, "Using Thesis Statements" (July 9, 2005), www.utoronto.ca/writing/thesis.html. Provides examples of good and bad thesis statements.

Assessment Tools

1. To reinforce what students have learned about the narrowing and thesis-development processes, have them narrow a topic by applying one or more of the narrowing strategies in chapter 1. Then have them formulate a rough thesis.

2. Have each student write three different versions of his or her thesis. To help students strategize, provide them with models from the thesis templates in examples 2.2–2.4.

3. See example 2.4 for an exercise in which students evaluate thesis statements. This exercise also can be used as an in-class exercise; it includes an instructor's discussion guide.

APPENDIX: EXAMPLES

Example 2.1: Sample Thesis Statements

Note: These thesis statements respond to the topic development examples in chapter 1 (examples 1.1–1.12).

Topic: American Indians
Thesis: "The increased violence in California's mining communities was an indication that cultural differences were creating racial tensions."[3]

Topic: Hazing
Thesis: "Alcohol abuse and hazing are closely related and must be addressed as addictions."[4]

Topic: Faith-Based Initiatives
Thesis: "Current statutes and policies that discriminate against the religious viewpoints of [faith-based organizations] have the effect of suppressing their unique character and risk alienating them entirely from participating in government programs."[5]

Topic: Toni Morrison's *Beloved*
Thesis: Toni Morrison, in her novel *Beloved*, develops the idea that maternal bonds can stunt or even obviate a woman's individuation or sense of self.[6]

Topic: Private Contractors in Iraq
Thesis: "The military's use of contractors saves taxpayers money and improves efficiency by freeing up soldiers for strictly combat operations."[7]

Example 2.2: Argumentative Theses, Templates

1. It is my claim in this paper that _____.
2. Some experts argue that _____, but I suggest _____ _____.
3. Although studies have documented _____, I contend that _____.
4. Most scholars agree that _____, but I propose an alternative [reading, interpretation, theory].
5. I analyze the debate concerning _____, and I suggest that _____.
6. Few [historians, scientists, scholars, critics,] to date have looked at _____. I attempt to fill this gap by considering _____.
7. I challenge assumptions about _____ and argue _____.
8. In an attempt to move the debate beyond discussions of _____ _____, this paper argues for _____.

9. Scholars vigorously debate _____. In this paper I argue that _____.

10. This paper presents the results of _____, which provides evidence that _____.

Example 2.3: Descriptive Theses, Templates

1. I examine debates provoked by _____.

2. The most contentious issue among scholars of _____ may be the _____.

3. This paper discusses the benefits and limitations of _____.

4. This paper surveys the clash between those who _____ and those who _____.

5. This paper describes _____'s career as _____.

6. This paper surveys the debates over the relationships between _____ and _____.

7. While I do not add to this debate, I discuss _____ that frames it and how _____ has provoked controversy from all sides.

8. This paper aims to describe and account for _____.

9. Through a series of short case studies, this article explores _____.

Example 2.4: Thesis Statement Exercise

Criteria for a good thesis:

1. Does it have a topic and an assertion?
2. Is it specific?
3. Can the thesis be substantiated?
4. Is the information accurate?

Are each of the following statements a thesis? If yes, are they well developed? Could they be improved? How? If you decide a statement is not a thesis, explain why.

1. In today's society, child abuse is an awful thing.
2. Some kinds of mining interfere with an area.
3. Smoking damages the body.
4. Lots of people die from handguns.
5. What are the major characteristics of adult children of alcoholics?
6. Laughter can cure many problems.
7. People should not smoke because it is unhealthy.
8. Although it has long been said that marriage is a woman's dream and a man's nightmare, recent studies show that men benefit more from the stability and companionship of marriage than women do.
9. Many researchers disagree as to whether alcoholism is a disease or a habit.
10. Who will commit crimes is largely determined by their surroundings.

Example 2.5: Thesis Statement, Instructor's Guide

Criteria for a good thesis:

1. Does it have a topic and an assertion?
2. Is it specific?
3. Can the thesis be substantiated?
4. Is the information accurate?

This exercise can also be used as in-class exercise. Points of discussions are included for each of the following statements.

Are each of the following statements a thesis? If yes, are they well developed? Could they be improved? How? If you decide a statement is not a thesis, explain why.

1. In today's society, child abuse is an awful thing.
   Who would argue that child abuse is a good thing?
   Can you think of some areas of the child-abuse issue that are controversial?
2. Some kinds of mining interfere with an area.
   What makes this thesis vague? How can it be improved?
   Should we narrow to a specific kind of mining?

What does interfere *mean?*
Area *is too vague. How can it be specified?*

3. Smoking damages the body.
   What makes this thesis vague?
   What is meant by damages?
   Should it be narrowed to a particular organ or body part?

4. Lots of people die from handguns.
   How can this statement be converted to an argumentative thesis?
   What controversies are associated with handgun ownership?

5. What are the major characteristics of adult children of alcoholics?
   While this is a research question, how can it be developed into a thesis?

6. Laughter can cure many problems.
   How can this vague statement be improved?
   What parts need to be more specific?
   Is the assertion strong enough?

7. People should not smoke because it is unhealthy.
   This is an example of a "so what" thesis. How can it be developed into a more controversial statement?

8. Although it has long been said that marriage is a woman's dream and a man's nightmare, recent studies show that men benefit more from the stability and companionship of marriage than women do.
   This is a well-defined thesis. What makes this a good thesis?
   How does it differ from the vague theses previously discussed?

9. Many researchers disagree as to whether alcoholism is a disease or a habit.
   While this is a descriptive thesis, how can it be converted to an argumentative thesis?

10. Who will commit crimes is largely determined by their surroundings.
    Why is this thesis vague?
    How can it be developed into a stronger statement?

NOTES

1. Ambrose Bierce, *The Enlarged Devil's Dictionary* (Garden City, NY: Doubleday, 1943), 47.
2. William Hazlitt, "Miscellaneous Writings" in *The Complete Works of William Hazlitt*, vol. 20, ed. P. P. Howe (New York: AMS, 1967), 309.
3. Howard Dewitt, "The Gold Rush and California Statehood" in *The California Dream* (Dubuque, Iowa: Kendall/Hunt, 1997).
4. Barbara B. Hollmann, "Hazing: Hidden Campus Crime," *New Directions for Students Services* 99 (2002): 14.
5. V. R. Broyles, "The Faith-Based Initiative, Charitable Choice, Faith-Based Organizations," *Harvard Journal of Law and Public Policy* 26 (2003): 317.
6. Adapted from Stephanie A. Demetrakopoulos, "Maternal Bonds as Devourers of Women's Individuation in Toni Morrison's *Beloved*," *African American Review* 26 (1992): 51.
7. "Privatizing the Military," *CQ Researcher*, June 25, 2004, 565.

BASIC BOOLEAN SEARCH STRATEGIES

Most people have learned about [online] searching the way they
learned about sex—from their friends.[1]

Goal: To retrieve a set of highly relevant references.
Objective 1: Construct a Boolean search strategy.
Objective 2: Apply a Boolean strategy to locate resources in major
bibliographic databases.

Boolean operators[2] drive the search engines of most of the bibliographic databases licensed by academic libraries. As one librarian suggests, "Boolean operators are the basic tools, the hammers and saws, of
most of the information retrieval systems we use today."[3] Boolean is a
powerful search method that increases a searcher's precision in probing
the depths of electronic databases. But to harness the power of Boolean
searching, the searcher must know how to control and manipulate its
powerful operators.

As powerful as Boolean is as a searching method, it is not readily appre-
ciated by novice searchers. "Why," they ask, "do we need Boolean when
we have Google and Yahoo?" To understand students' initial resistance

to Boolean, it is essential to first understand their culture. Most college-bound students have been weaned on the Internet, which they perceive as a vast repository, rich in information that can be instantly retrieved by a few keystrokes. This omnipotent view is reinforced by the media, parents, and teachers, who encourage them to use the Internet to research their school projects as well as to entertain themselves.

Granted, the Internet has allowed students access to new and heretofore inaccessible information sources, but today's cyberspace has also engendered a false sense of security in terms of the ability to search for meaningful information. Media hype and easy access to the Internet seduces the untrained into believing that searching need not be a high-level skill: one simply plugs in a word or string of words. Students are pragmatists. They prefer methods of searching that are simple and straightforward, have few complexities, and include a formula that can be applied to any situation. Or, some seek a prescription-free approach in which no rules apply.

While it may be true that unsystematic searching works quite successfully with some topics, usually it is these that do not require a set of relationships or are for personal use, such as a biopic of a rock star. However, natural language or simple keyword searching often proves clumsy when applied to college-level topics, which typically deal with multiple concepts or variables. Unsystematic searching, therefore, may meet the immediate needs of the searcher, but such methods prove chaotic and frustrating when the search fails to yield satisfactory results. Worse still, if a search yields unsatisfactory results, unskilled searchers often fall into the trap of assuming that nothing exists on their topic. In learning alternative strategies, students will be less likely to make such erroneous assumptions and will enjoy an overall richer experience.

Another factor of student resistance to systematic searching is their lack of problem-solving skills. This deficiency in problem solving is supported by several studies that indicate elementary and high school students have difficulty developing search statements that reflect a topic to be searched, identifying major concepts, and assigning synonyms to these concepts. Problem solving is grounded in three basic thinking processes: analysis, synthesis, and creativity. Students trained in these processes will be better able to conceptualize an appropriate search statement for academic-oriented topics.

The conceptual approach can be intimidating to students; it forces them to observe and construct their world in ways far different from what they are comfortable with. The challenge for librarian-instructors is to present the idea so that students will relinquish their preconceived notions of searching and buy into the conceptual approach. And once students have embraced the conceptual approach, it is the less likely that their preconceived notions will interfere with the goals and objectives of the course.

LEARNING OBJECTIVES AND INSTRUCTOR ACTIVITIES

The best way to teach students how to construct Boolean search strategies is to have them learn the Boolean process sequentially:

1. Write a clear statement of the topic.
2. Divide the topic into concepts.
3. Select words to express each concept.
4. Use truncation appropriately.
5. Translate the Boolean strategy into a parenthetical statement.

After the statement is created, apply a Boolean search strategy to relevant library databases. This strategy should be used in conjunction with the search strategies in chapter 5.

Objective 1: Construct a Boolean Search Strategy.

Step 1: Write a Clear Statement of the Topic. Defining a research problem and writing a clear statement of it challenges many students because reducing a problem to a single statement requires focused thinking. To help students conceptualize effective search statements, the instructor should encourage them to write a search statement in the form of a phrase, question, or thesis/hypothesis. For example:

phrase: violent TV programs and violent behavior in little kids
question: Does watching violent TV programs cause violent behavior in
little kids?

thesis: Watching violent TV programs causes violent behavior in little kids.

The stage at which the student is in the research process, however, often dictates the type of statement employed. For example, if students are just beginning to explore a topic, they may not have enough background to write a thesis or hypothesis. In this case, students should try to express their topic statement in the form of a phrase or question. On the other hand, students who have done background research on their topic may be in a better position to write a more complex statement, such as a thesis or hypothesis. For discussions on framing questions and developing theses, see chapters 1 and 2 respectively.

Students, however, need to be aware that some thesis statements must be broken into components and constructed as separate search strategies. This is especially true for issue-based theses where several sides are represented in a research project. The thesis "The system of delivering death sentences is fair and reliable" is a typical example of a thesis used in lower-division composition papers. A preliminary search strategy could be constructed like so (truncation ignored):

death penalty OR capital punishment OR death sentences
AND
fair OR reliable

While this search is logically stated and will retrieve relevant material, it will not retrieve a number of relevant items because it fails to adequately represent the several arguments associated with the death penalty issue. To retrieve these arguments, the student should link the death penalty concept with a concept that reflects one aspect of the debate, for example, the racial implications of the death sentence.

death penalty OR capital punishment OR death sentence
AND
racial OR ethnicity OR minorities

This search query will target those items that specifically deal with arguments of race, whereas the documents from the first search may just touch upon the death penalty.

Step 2: Divide the Topic into Concepts. Once the search statement is constructed, it must then deconstructed. This second step in the Boolean search process requires the searcher to identify the major concepts of the search statement. To help students identify the major concepts, the instructor encourages them to ask, "What words (i.e., concepts) in this statement are the most important?"

Scenario:

INSTRUCTOR: [writes this topic statement on the board: "Does watching violent TV programs cause violent behavior in little kids?"] What is one concept that is important?
STUDENTS: TV programs.
INSTRUCTOR: Do you want all articles on TV or only those that relate to . . . ?
STUDENTS: Violence.
INSTRUCTOR: Okay, so you do you want all articles on TV and violence or only those that include . . . ?
STUDENTS: Kids.

Asking these questions encourages students to learn to think in terms of conceptual relationships and to separate the essential words from "fluff" words that interfere with the success of a search. Fluff words increases the possibility of either retrieving false hits or eliminating important references. The failure to eliminate unnecessary words can seriously derail a search.

Identifying fluff words is one of the most challenging aspects of Boolean concept formation. Inexperienced students include fluff words because they *seem* to be concepts. Typical words that masquerade as concepts include: effect, implication, controversy, or relationship. For example, when identifying the major concepts of the search query "What is the relationship between stress and depression?" many students will select "relationship" along with "depression" and "stress." This is an incorrect Boolean statement. Yet, students will argue that they retrieved some "good stuff," and they are correct to a limited degree. But, what they do not realize is they are also *missing* a core of highly relevant items because the word *relationship* is not explicitly stated only implied. That is, one does not need to use *relationship* because it is implied when *depression* is combined with *stress*. Thus, the relationship between depression and stress is expressed indirectly.

Step 3: Select Words to Express Each Concept. Assigning synonyms or closely related words to concepts presents another set of challenges for the novice searcher. Inexperienced searchers assume that if they enter a word expressing the concept "teen" for example, the computer will retrieve all records dealing with the population group aged thirteen to nineteen. Yet, as experienced searchers know, if other appropriate terms are not included (e.g., *adolescents*) many relevant references will be dropped from the search results.

Scenario:

INSTRUCTOR: A student enters the phrase "old people" but retrieves very few articles. Why? Because few scholars will use that phrase to express that concept. What might they use instead?

STUDENTS: Senior citizens, elderly, geriatric.

INSTRUCTOR: Good. But you have overlooked an important term used in citations to books and articles: *aged*. Let's take another example. If you only enter the words *little kids* when connecting it to TV and violence you will retrieve very few articles. Why? Because *kids* is an informal word that most professional authors will not use. Instead, they will use words such as . . .

STUDENTS: Children?

INSTRUCTOR: What else? Think of how scholars and researchers would describe little kids.

STUDENTS: Preschoolers? Toddlers?

INSTRUCTOR: Right. So in your search strategy, you will include *children* OR *preschoolers* OR *toddlers*.

Assigning synonyms to a concept can be challenging to novice searchers because they lack the breadth of knowledge to readily identify the various terms that can be used to express a concept. To find synonyms, students tend to turn to an online thesaurus. While this reference can be of some use, it often suggests terms that are less than helpful. For example, J. I. Rodale's *The Synonym Finder*[4] lists for *old age* such terms as *declining years, oldness, antiquity*. While these terms signify old age, they are not the types of terms that researchers and scholars use to discuss the elderly. Instead of relying solely on dictionaries, students should form the habit of observing, through their background reading and search results, the words and phrases used by authors and scholars to express particular concepts. Students should keep a running record of these keywords and use them when developing search strategies.

Step 4: Use Truncation Appropriately.   Truncation seems an easy concept to grasp, but it stumps many novice searchers. One reason is that many students lack adequate skills in spelling and knowledge of variant forms of words. For example, inexperienced students will most likely truncate the word *disabled* as "disabl*," unaware that this version will not retrieve its variants *disability* or *disabilities*.

A second problem is students cut too far into the word—*agricultural* as "ag*," which retrieves a host of irrelevant words, such as *age, aged, aggregate*, and *agrarian*. Yet, in other situations, students fail to truncate at all and stick the symbol behind a complete word. This often occurs with plurals, for example, "dogs*" or "planets*."

Finally, students misapply truncation when they fail to consider the meaning of words. For example, they will truncate *sexism* as "sex*," not realizing that this will bring a great deal of irrelevant hits that have nothing to do with sexist behavior.

While practice and experience will prevent students from making truncation errors, they should also be encouraged to rely less on guessing where to truncate and more on a good dictionary to determine variants of words.

Step 5: Translate the Boolean Strategy into a Parenthetical Statement.   Learning to write parenthetical statements enables students to understand the relationships between the Boolean operators AND and OR. For example,

(tv OR television) AND (children OR toddlers OR preschoolers) AND (violence OR aggression OR antisocial)

Discussing examples of parenthetical statements can help students avoid misusing AND and OR operators

1. *(homeless AND alcoholism) OR (cocaine OR heroin)*   While this search will retrieve items on alcoholic homeless people, it will also bring back all articles where the words *cocaine* and *heroin* appear. Thus, a more appropriate search strategy would look like this:

homeless AND (alcoholism OR cocaine OR heroin)

2. depression AND teenagers AND adolescents   This statement reflects an incorrect use of AND. The novice searcher thinks he or she is requesting all articles on dealing with depressed teens or adolescents. However, the computer interprets the request quite differently. It retrieves only those records on depression that contain the *teenagers* and *adolescents*. Thus, a more effective statement would look like this:

depression AND (teenagers OR adolescents)

3. Aztecs AND gods OR religion AND fertility   This confused statement shows students that parentheses are necessary to make the relationships clear. The better statement would look like this:

Aztecs AND (gods OR religion) AND fertility

It is advisable to refrain from teaching the third Boolean operator NOT until students have some experience with AND and OR. While the NOT operator can be very powerful, inexperienced searchers often misunderstand its function. Though the NOT operator eliminates a concept, it may also drop relevant documents.

Objective 2: Apply a Boolean Strategy to Locate Resources in Major Bibliographic Databases.

While the delivery of the demonstration depends on the type of instructional session and teaching facility, students should already be familiar with the content and structure of the database. For an in-depth discussion of periodical literature, see chapter 4, and for searching periodical databases, see chapter 5.

CLASS ACTIVITIES

For specific activities in the classroom, refer to the chapters dealing with searching periodical databases (chapter 5), online public access catalogs (OPACs; chapter 7), and the Internet (chapter 9). Whatever activity is used to teach Boolean and other search strategies, students should be provided a worksheet or planner to help them work through the search strategy process. Also have students develop their own cheat sheets when learning search steps and protocols; they reinforce skills and provide guides for future searches.

INSTRUCTOR GUIDES, HANDOUTS, AND EXERCISES

1. Example 3.1: Boolean Search Strategy, A Checklist
2. Example 3.2: Boolean Operators, A Brief Guide
3. Examples 3.3–3.4: Venn Diagrams, exercise and answer key
4. Examples 3.5–3.8: Search Strategies, exercises and answer keys
5. Examples 3.9–3.10: Synonym/Truncation, exercise and answer key
6. Example 3.11: Search Strategy, Worksheet

Websites on Boolean Operators and Venn Diagrams

1. California State University, Hayward Library, "Boolean Operators: Key Aids in Developing Effective Search Strategies," www.library.csuhayward.edu/staff/highsmith/BooleanOperators.htm. Provides a one-page guide on using Boolean operators.
2. Beverley Choltco-Devlin, "Boolean Guides and Exercises" (May 2002), www.midyork.org/home/search/boolean_principals.html. Provides a Boolean logic guide, concept analysis worksheet, and exercise on constructing Boolean search statements.
3. K. Davies, "A Lesson in Boolean Logic, Simpsons-Style" (July 16, 2001), library.geneseo.edu/~davies/LessonBooleanLogic.pdf.
4. Duke University Libraries, "Electronic Searching" (July 14, 2003), www.lib.duke.edu/libguide/adv_searching.htm. Chart includes explanations and examples for Boolean operators and proximity searching.
5. InfoPeople Project, "Best Search Tools Chart" (2006), www.infopeople.org/search/chart.html. Chart includes search engines that provide Boolean capabilities.
6. Lake Sumter Community College Library, "Boolean Search Guide" (April 24, 2004), www.lscc.cc.fl.us/library/guides/boolsea.htm. Graphical guide includes tips on proximity searching.

7. Library of Congress, "Boolean Searching Chart" (September 3, 2003, catalog.loc.gov/help/boolean.htm.
8. New York University Libraries, "Tutorial: Boolean Searching," library.nyu.edu/research/health/tutorial/boolean.htm. Provides a graphical chart explaining basic Boolean operators and how each affects a search.
9. State University of New York, Albany Library, "A Primer in Boolean Logic" (May 2006), www.internettutorials.net/boolean.html. A graphical tutorial that includes applying Boolean to Internet searching.
10. University of Helsinki, "Searching Information," www.opiskelijakirjasto.lib.helsinki.fi/koulutus/libtut/index.html. Provides detailed tutorial on search strategies.
11. Western Michigan University, "Searchpath," wwwmail.wnec.edu/library. Tutorial includes exercises.

Assessment Tools

1. American University Library, "Search Strategies: Boolean Operators," www.library.american.edu/tutorial/keyword5.html. Tutorial includes interactive Boolean exercises.
2. Joe Barker, University of California, Berkeley, "Topic Worksheet" (2004), www.lib.berkeley.edu/TeachingLib/Guides/Internet/Boolean.pdf.
3. Beverley Choltco-Devlin, "Boolean Guides and Exercises" (May 20, 2004), www.midyork.org/home/search/boolean_principals. html. Provides a Boolean logic guide, concept analysis worksheet, and exercise on constructing Boolean search statements.
4. Creighton University Library, "Boolean Logic" (July 20, 2006), reinert.creighton.edu/resources/toolkit/boolean.htm. A strategy planner accompanies a brief Boolean explanation. The planner helps students construct a search statement based on their topic. Includes a sample planner.
5. Humboldt State University Library, "Electronic Searching Quiz" (January 19, 2005), library.humboldt.edu/infoservices/OWLS/OWL4-Test.htm. Quizzes use Boolean operators and truncation.

6. McMaster University, Department of Social Sciences, "Locating Journals," socserv2.mcmaster.ca/Inquiry/LibraryExercise2.htm. Guided search exercise using Boolean operators.

7. Moravian College and Moravian Theological Seminary Library, "Searching for Periodical Articles," home.moravian.edu/public/reevestutorial/pages/Database/DATABASESintro.htm.

8. Purdue University, "CORE: Comprehensive Online Research Education" (February 14, 2006), gemini.lib.purdue.edu/core/default.cfm. Provides discussion on search basics and types of searches. Includes a pretest and quizzes.

9. Skyline College Library, "Lesson 7: Advanced Keyword Searching" (2004), www.smccd.net/accounts/skylib/lsci100/lesson.htm. Very detailed, graphic tutorial on Boolean searching. Includes a password-protected test.

10. South Australia, Department of Further Education, Employment, Science, and Technology, "LILI: Learn Information Literacy Initiative" (July 28, 2006), www2.tafe.sa.edu.au/lili/index. html. Provides a component on analyzing search statements and selecting keywords and concepts.

11. University of Alabama, "Introduction to Boolean Logic" (April 7, 2004), fc.eng.ua.edu/GES/?id=206. Includes detailed instruction in Boolean logic with graphics, quizzes and exercises, and individual and team assignments.

12. University of North Carolina Library, "Information Literacy Modules: Searching Databases and Evaluating Results," www.library. ncat.edu/ref/information_literacy/course/toc.htm. Tutorial includes examples drawn from EbscoHost and Infotrac. Includes quizzes.

13. University of Utah, Health Sciences Library, "Internet Navigator: Module 3," www-navigator.utah.edu. This interactive tutorial provides two tracks. Track 1 focuses on general topics, and track 2 is restricted to health-related topics. Provides assignments and quizzes. See module 2 for an interactive exercise on identifying keywords in thesis statements.

14. University of Washington, "Research 101," www.lib.washington. edu/uwill/research101/index.html. Includes components selecting keywords and concepts and creating Boolean search strategies accompanied by exercises and review quizzes.

15. West Virginia University College of Law, "Library, Boolean Logic Guide and Quiz" (December 5, 2005), www.wvu.edu/~law/library/guides/booleanquiz.htm. Tutorial provides a quiz.

APPENDIX: EXAMPLES

Example 3.1: Boolean Search Strategy, A Checklist

How Do I Begin?
1. Write a clear statement of topic.
2. Divide topic into concepts.
3. Select words to express each concept.
4. Truncate relevant words.
5. Select appropriate database.
6. Perform search.
7. Evaluate results.
9. Modify search if necessary.

What If I Retrieve No Articles or Irrelevant Stuff?
1. Check spelling.
2. Check the database—is it the best one for your topic?
3. Limit search to subject/title fields.
4. Rethink Boolean concepts.
5. Add or delete synonyms.
6. Reexamine truncation.

Example 3.2: Boolean Operators, A Brief Guide

Boolean AND operator
- Combines concepts. Each concept must be present in the results of the search.
- Example: recycle AND plastics
- Indicates that all references must contain the word *recycle* as well as the word *plastics*.
- The AND operator narrows and specifies the search.

Boolean OR operator
- Combines synonyms or closely related words and phrases.

- Example: recycle OR reuse
- Used to retrieve references that contain either the word *recycle* or the word *reuse*. The OR operator assumes that authors and indexers use different words and phrases to express a concept.
- The OR operator expands the search.

Boolean NOT operator

- Excludes concepts.
- Example: recycle NOT paper
- Includes *recycle* but excludes references that deal with recycling paper.
- The NOT operator narrows a search. This operator should be used carefully, as key articles may be excluded.

Example 3.3: Venn Diagrams, Exercise

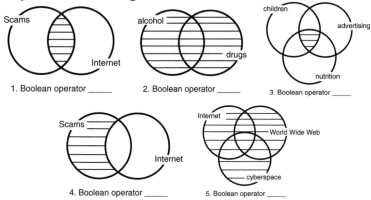

1. Boolean operator _____   2. Boolean operator _____   3. Boolean operator _____

4. Boolean operator _____   5. Boolean operator _____

Example 3.4: Venn Diagrams, Answer Key

1. AND   2. OR   3. AND   4. NOT   5. OR

Example 3.5: Search Strategies I, Exercise

Develop a Boolean search strategy for each of the following research questions. Include in your search strategy: key concepts, at least two synonyms for each concept, and truncation. Test all strategies in appropriate databases before you commit them to paper.

1. What are the effects of cocaine on areas of the brain?

2. What are the moral implications of marketing cigarettes?
3. What is the correlation between tobacco use and self-esteem?
4. What kind of criminal schemes involve stocks on the Internet?
5. What is the impact of global warming on wildlife in the polar regions?
6. Do food advertisements influence a child's diet?

Example 3.6: Search Strategies I, Answer Key

These are suggested search strategies and may not include all possible synonyms. This key does not provide answers to relevant databases, as these will vary widely among libraries. Note * is the symbol for truncation.

1. What are the effects of cocaine on areas of the brain?
   (cocaine OR crack) AND (brain OR cereb* or cognit*)
2. What are the moral implications of marketing cigarettes?
   (moral* OR ethic*) AND (market* OR advertis* OR sell*) AND (cigarette* OR tobacco OR smok*)
3. What is the correlation between tobacco use and self-esteem?
   (smok* OR tobacco OR cigarette*) AND (self esteem OR self respect OR self confiden*)
4. What kind of criminal schemes involve stocks on the Internet?
   (crim* OR fraud* OR scam*) AND (stock* OR bond* OR securities) AND (Internet OR Web OR online OR cyber*)
5. What is the impact of global warming on wildlife in the polar regions?
   (global warming OR greenhouse) AND (wildlife OR animal* OR mammal* OR bird*) AND (polar OR arctic* OR antarctic*)
6. Do food advertisements influence a child's diet?
   (food* OR diet* OR nutrition*) AND (child* OR toddler* OR preschool*) AND (advertis* OR market* OR ads)

Example 3.7: Search Strategies II, Exercise

Develop a Boolean search strategy for each of the following search statements. Include: key concepts, at least two synonyms for each concept, and truncation. Test all strategies in the appropriate database before you commit them to paper.

1. What are the real issues relating to kids going hungry in the United States?
2. Locate articles on women and the vote in Great Britain.
3. What is the relationship between teens using drugs and delinquency?
4. Some estimates indicate that the elderly commit a quarter of all suicides. A great proportion of these elderly who attempt or commit suicide have problems with excessive drinking.
5. Is TV violence to be blamed for the increased aggression in teens?
6. Find articles that discuss the negative images of overweight people.

Example 3.8: Search Strategies II, Answer Key

These are suggested search strategies and may not include all possible synonyms. This key does not provide answers to relevant databases, as these will vary widely among libraries. Note * is the symbol for truncation.

1. What are the real issues relating to kids going hungry in the United States?
   (infant* OR child* OR toddler* or preschool*) AND (hunger OR hungry OR malnourish* OR malnutrition* OR food shortage*) AND (United States OR U.S. OR America*)
2. Locate articles on women and the vote in Great Britain.
   (wom?n* OR female* OR femin*) AND (vot* OR suffrag*) AND (Brit* OR Engl*)
3. What is the relationship between teens using drugs and delinquency?
   (teen* OR adolesc* OR youth* OR high school*) AND (drug* OR crack OR marijuana) AND (delinq* OR crim* OR felon*)
4. Some estimates indicate that the elderly commit a quarter of all suicides. A great proportion of these elderly who attempt or commit suicide have problems with excessive drinking.

(elder* OR aged OR senior citizen*) AND (suicid* OR self murder* OR self destruct*) AND (drink* OR drunk* OR alcohol*)

5. Is TV violence to be blamed for the increased aggression in teens?
(tv OR televis*) AND (violen* OR aggress*) AND (teen* OR adolesc* OR youth* OR high school*)

6. Find articles that discuss the negative images of overweight people.

Example 3.9: Synonym/Truncation, Exercise

I. Synonyms   To search successfully, you must think of words so close in meaning to your concept words that they might have been used in the title or in the indexing of an article on your topic. Try these:

Example: adolescent OR teenager

1. careers OR_____OR_____
2. firearms OR_____OR_____
3. old people OR_____OR _____
4. women OR _____
5. death penalty OR _____OR _____
6. cats OR _____OR _____
7. high schools OR _____

II. Truncation   Where should we truncate? If we cut off too much of the word, we may retrieve other words that have nothing to do with our subject. If we don't cut off enough, we may miss some forms of our word. List all possible variants of words.

Example: industries
two variants of word: industry, industrial
truncated form: industr*

1. parents
three variants of word:
truncated form:

2. pollute
   four variants of word:
   truncated form:
3. stereotype
   four variants of word:
   truncated form:
4. sexists
   two variants of word:
   truncated form:
5. vehicles
   two variants of word:
   truncated form:

Example 3.10: Synonym/Truncation, Answer Key

I. Synonyms To search successfully, you must think of words so close in meaning to your concept words that they might have been used in the title or in the indexing of an article on your topic. Try these:

1. careers OR jobs OR vocations
2. firearms OR guns OR handguns OR rifles
3. old people OR elderly OR aged OR senior citizens
4. women OR females
5. death penalty OR death sentence OR capital punishment
6. cats OR felines OR kittens
7. high schools OR secondary schools

II. Truncation Where should we truncate? If we cut off too much of the word, we may retrieve other words that have nothing to do with our subject. If we don't cut off enough, we may miss some forms of our word. List all possible variants of words.

1. parents
   three variants of word: parent, parental, parenting
   truncated form: parent*
2. pollute
   four variants of word: polluted, pollutes, polluting, pollutant

truncated form: pollut*
3. stereotype
   four variants of word: stereotypes, stereotyped, stereotyping, stereotypical
   truncated form: stereotyp*
4. sexists
   two variants of word: sexist, sexism
   truncated form: sexis*
5. vehicles
   two variants of word: vehicle, vehicular
   truncated form: vehic*

Example 3.11: Search Strategy, Worksheet

1. Develop a statement of your topic.
2. Divide the topic statement into concepts.
3. Select synonyms that express each concept.
4. Choose appropriate research databases.
5. Apply search strategy to the database.

NOTES

1. Rita Vine, "Real People Don't Do Boolean," *Information Outlook*, March 2001, 18.
2. British mathematician George Boole developed Boolean logic decades before the advent of computers. Computing experts discovered that his logic was very adaptable to computer programming.
3. Douglas Morton, "Refresher Course: Boolean AND (Searching OR Retrieval)," *Online*, January 1993, 57.
4. J. I. Rodale, *The Synonym Finder* (New York: Warner, 1986), 805.

4

EVALUATING
PERIODICAL LITERATURE

Some [literary men] were selling their souls to the periodical press.[1]

Goal: To recognize what a periodical is and its importance in research.

Objective 1: Define a periodical.

Objective 2: Identify types of periodicals and their levels of authority.

Objective 3: Understand the editorial perspectives.

Many college instructors require that students cite only scholarly periodicals in their term projects and often express this requirement in their syllabuses with such phrases as: "academic periodicals," "professional journals," "periodicals of a scholarly nature," or "research journals." While this requirement is quite clear to experienced researchers, novice students become confused as to what is wanted or assume that "academic periodicals" means anything that is available via the university library. Consequently, they are susceptible to accessing unsatisfactory sources in the vein of *Society*, *Psychology Today*, and *National Geographic*. Whether you are teaching a one-shot session or an entire course never assume the students—lower division as well as upper division—know the definition of a periodical or can differentiate between the types of periodicals.

LEARNING OBJECTIVES AND INSTRUCTOR ACTIVITIES

Objective 1: Define a Periodical.

Scenario:

> INSTRUCTOR: What is a periodical?
> STUDENT A: It's a magazine.
> STUDENT B: Yeah. Something like *Newsweek.*
> INSTRUCTOR: Yes, *Newsweek* is a periodical, but what makes *Newsweek* a periodical?
> STUDENTS: [blank looks]

Describing what makes a periodical a periodical stumps many students. Ironically, while most have been exposed to periodicals all their lives, they are stymied when asked to differentiate them from other types of sources. The following section begins with the definition of a periodical and then proceeds to flesh out some of its salient features.

Features of Periodicals: The Periodical versus the Scholarly Monograph.   A periodical can be defined as a publication that is issued at regular intervals. Its regularity distinguishes it from the monograph, which deals with a single subject and is published once (unless it is revised or reprinted). Moreover, the scope of a periodical article is very different from that of a monograph; the former treats a topic narrowly, while the latter treats it globally. For example, let's examine how a scholarly periodical and scholarly monograph treat the topic of personal ads on the Internet. An article in the *American Sociological Review* might focus on what women want versus what men want based on their preferences, whereas a monograph might provide a historical context and an in-depth analysis of the various facets of cyber-matchmaking.

Periodicals Are the Great Communicators.   Periodicals communicate current events, trends, and research much faster than books.

Exposing others to one's research findings is much quicker in periodicals than books. Some disciplines, especially the sciences, emphasize periodicals because scholars can readily share their ideas, experiments, theories, and discoveries with colleagues.

Periodicals Expose the New and Different. Periodicals often break stories that are arcane, provocative, or newfangled, such as biofouling, the South Beach Diet, and metrosexuals.

Periodicals Provide a Forum for Controversy. Each periodical claims an editorial stance that offers readers an opportunity to explore diverse perspectives—moral, social, political, and racial. For example, facts and opinions about the rights of Palestinians are reported differently according to the editorial position of the magazine. The following is a brief list of magazines and their political or social stances:

- *Tikkun* (Jewish perspective)
- *Arab American News* (Arab perspective)
- *Newsweek* (somewhat middle of the road)
- *National Review* (conservative)
- *The Nation* (liberal)
- *Reason* (libertarian)
- *Monthly Review* (socialist)

One of the best tools to determine the political position of a periodical is Katz's *Magazines for Libraries* and, for lesser-known periodicals, *The International Directory of Little Magazines and Small Presses*. In addition, the website of a periodical will often state its political perspective via the "About Us" link.

Objective 2: Identify Types of Periodicals and Their Levels of Authority.

While all periodicals have some properties in common, specific types of periodicals vary greatly in their audience, content, and purpose. Although students might be aware of the categorical differences of periodicals (e.g., newspapers, magazines, and scholarly journals), they assume that the authority of the articles is relative. That is, students give as much authoritative weight to *National Geographic* articles as those in the venerable *American Anthropologist*. While there are many distinctions between popular and scholarly, the major one to emphasize is that newspapers, trade periodicals, and magazines are not held to the same standards of documentation as scholarly journals. For instance, a reporter for the *Washington Post* can get away with citing "anonymous congressional sources" or "sources close to the Pentagon," yet a biologist writing for *Nature* could not cite "several anonymous cell biologists." While popular magazines and the trades are held to a looser standard in the attribution of facts and sources, the scholarly press is not—it is expected to produce full documentation to support facts, assertions, refutations, and conclusions.

The following section delineates the major periodical types that students will most likely encounter in their research.

Nonscholarly Press

Newspapers Newspapers report day-to-day events, trends, and issues and include feature articles, editorials, opinion polls, graphics, and advertisements. They are very useful in announcing the release of new scholarly studies, polls, and surveys and in determining the date an event occurred.

The following are examples of national newspapers:

- *Boston Globe*
- *Chicago Sun Times*
- *Christian Science Monitor*
- *Houston Chronicle*
- *Los Angeles Times*
- *New York Times*
- *Sacramento Bee*
- *Wall Street Journal*
- *Washington Post*[2]

Popular Magazines Popular magazines are usually published weekly, biweekly, or monthly; are geared to a specific niche (news and commentary, intellectual and cultural life, the arts, hobbies, fashion, and gossip); and whose editorial content may inform, explain, interpret, comment, or advocate. The following are popular magazines in order of authority.

Magazines that report the news and discuss sociopolitical problems, the arts, and intellectual concerns are considered the top tier of the hierarchy of popular magazines. However, many in this category fail to meet social historian Russell Lynes's definition of *highbrow*.[3] These newsweeklies and magazines aim to contribute to serious public discourse with in-depth reporting, analysis, and criticism on the issues and problems facing society. Some of these publications survive not by selling advertising but by relying on subscriptions, donations, and grants. While biased reporting exists, most of these periodicals attempt to adhere to journalistic standards of objectivity and factual reporting. However, while some sourcing can be independently verified, many stories are based on anonymous or secondhand sources. Regardless of how the sources are reported, there are no formal citations as in scholarly journals. Yet, for research, newsweeklies and periodicals on intellectual and cultural affairs are rich in research possibilities:

- They keep abreast of political, social, and cultural news.
- They use primary materials in historical research.
- They provide deep background into complex topics.

These are some examples of some well-known periodicals:

- *American Spectator* (www.spectator.org)
- *The Atlantic* (www.theatlantic.com)
- *Economist* (www.economist.co.uk)
- *Harper's Magazine* (www.harpers.com)
- *Humanist* (www.thehumanist.org)
- *Mother Jones* (www.motherjones.com)
- *The Nation* (www.thenation.com)
- *National Geographic* (www.nationalgeographic.com)
- *National Review* (www.nationalreview.com)
- *New Criterion* (www.newcriterion.com)
- *New Republic* (www.tnr.com)
- *New Yorker* (www.newyorker.com)
- *Newsweek* (www.msnbc.msn.com)
- *Slate* (www.slate.com)
- *Time* (www.time.com/time)
- *Utne Magazine* (www.utne.com/pub)

Following are examples of databases that include well-known periodicals:

- *Academic Search Elite (EbscoHost)*
- *Academic Search Premier (EbscoHost)*
- *Expanded Academic ASAP*
- *Lexis/Nexis Academic*
- *Reader's Guide Full Text (WilsonWeb)*[4]

Entertainment and Style   These magazines emphasize celebrity, fashion, style, and trendy products. Exorbitant amounts of money are spent on splashy layouts and advertising to entice readers to buy their products. But, beneath the hype and color, the editorial content is shallow and expressed in simple language. These magazines have very little research value, however students may use them for inspiration. For example, *Vogue's* "Age Issue" may inspire students to develop topics, such as "middle-aged women adjusting to physical changes brought about by aging" or "age stereotypes in older and younger women."
Following are some examples of entertainment and style magazines:

- *Entertainment Weekly*
- *GQ*
- *People Weekly*
- *Vogue*

The following are examples of databases that include entertainment magazines:

- *Academic Search Elite (EbscoHost)*
- *Expanded Academic ASAP*
- *Lexis/Nexis Academic*
- *Reader's Guide Full Text (WilsonWeb)*

Supermarket Tabloids   Nearly everyone has read the *National Enquirer* or *Star*—but few admit to it. Historically, the tabloids have been ostracized from the mainstream press for their "trashy" coverage of politicians, celebrities, crime, and the ubiquitous aliens from outer space.

But the mainstream press no longer can ignore the tabs; since the 1980s, they have broken big stories that have affected the careers of politicians and influenced the outcome of criminal trials. For example, *Star* first exposed the alleged affair between Gennifer Flowers and President Bill Clinton. And the *National Enquirer* published a photograph of O. J. Simpson wearing Bruno Magli shoes—which he denied owning—that served as a key piece of evidence in the civil suit brought against him by the victims' families. Moreover, *Time* named Steve Coz, editor of the *National Enquirer*, as one of America's twenty-five most influential people.[5] Gone are the days when the mainstream press could write off the tabs as nothing but "sex, gore, and bizarre tales of human behavior."[6] The barrier between the tabs and the mainstream press appears to be gone, and, as a result, "the cultures of entertainment, infotainment, argument, analyses, tabloid and mainstream press not only work side by side but intermingle and merge."[7] This "mixed media" environment has been created because market forces have compelled the mainstream media to compete with the tabloids for attention-grabbing headlines; thus, competition for audiences has relaxed traditional newsgathering standards and practices. The mainstream press no longer decides what is news.

While the tabloids are negligible in terms of research due to stories based on questionable reporting standards, sensationalized stories can lead to serious questions. For example, stories surrounding Bill Clinton and Monica Lewinsky could be used as a springboard for studying the meaning of lying or the ethics of exposing the private lives of politicians. Here are some examples of tabloid magazines:

- *National Enquirer* (www.nationalenquirer.com)
- *Star Magazine* (www.starmagazine.com)[8]

Trade/Professional Magazines   Positioned between general interest magazines and scholarly journals, trade magazines focus on a specific profession (archaeology or biology) or industry (biotechnology or advertising). Unlike peer-reviewed journals, trade articles focus less on the scholar and more on the practitioner who strives to be more aware, productive, and effective in his or her profession or business. Consequently, trade magazines review and analyze products and techniques, highlight the latest news and trends, and introduce new practices and technologies. Writers contributing to the trades may be scholars and practitioners trained in the field or authors who have developed a good reputation within the professional or trade community. For research purposes, trade publications can help researchers to identify hot topics and new innovations and to seek out solutions to problems. The following are examples of trade magazines:

- *Advertising Age* (www.adage.com)
- *Archaeology* (www.archaeology.org)
- *Editor & Publisher* (www.editorandpublisher.com/eandp/index.jsp)
- *History Today* (www.historytoday.com)
- *New Scientist* (www.newscientist.com)
- *Psychology Today* (cms.psychologytoday.com/pto/home.php)
- *Science News* (www.sciencenews.org)
- *Scientific American* (www.sciam.com)
- *Society* (www.transaction.com)

The following are examples of databases that include trade magazines:

- *ABI/Inform*
- *Academic Search Elite (EbscoHost)*
- *Academic Search Premier (EbscoHost)*
- *Expanded Academic ASAP*
- *Lexis/Nexis Academic*
- *Omnifile Full Text (WilsonWeb)*

Note that some specialized databases will index professional magazines. For example *America: History & Life* includes *History Today* in its database.

Alternative Press   Born into the activism of the 1960s, the alternative press emerged to expose the news and voices that have been downplayed, distorted, or ignored by the established press because of fear of alienating corporate heads, advertisers, or readers. Consider this recent example. According to Carl Jensen and Peter Phillips, the American mainstream press "ducked and covered" from reporting that the United States destroyed Iraq's water supply during the 1991 Gulf War and prevented efforts to rebuild the water system after the war.[9] In September 2000, the *Sunday Herald* (Scotland) broke the story, followed by a brief article in the *Orlando Sentinel* and an in-depth article written by Thomas J. Nagy for the alternative *The Progressive*. Subsequently, only the *Capital Times* (Madison) and the *National Catholic Reporter* reported on the findings of Nagy's article.[10]

Alternative magazines provide readers with divergent perceptions, points of view, and explanations of social, political, and economic issues. Encouraging students to supplement their research with alternative articles enables them to acknowledge that many issues are inherently complex and thinking about them through a black/white or either/or mindset clouds sound reasoning, judgment, and an appreciation for divergent views. Moreover, students can become vicarious learners by going beyond articles in the mainstream to examine points of view that may seem alien to them. Consider the topic of school prayer. Students can learn the arguments put forth by atheists in *American Atheist*, by libertarians in *Reason*, by socialists in *Monthly Review*, and by followers of Pat Buchanan in the *American Conservative*.

Further, students can learn through the voices of people who come from different racial and ethnic backgrounds than themselves. The points of views, perceptions, and opinions of blacks, Hispanics, Asian Americans, American Indians, Arab Americans, and Jews, which often are invisible in the mainstream press, can provide additional contexts from which to understand a topic. For example, students who critique the black male experience in film may run the risk of stereotyping if they base their evidence solely on movie reviews written by mainstream critics. Yet, the critique will be much more authentic if the student researches the perceptions of critics writing for the black press and other alternative publications. Listed are examples of alternative magazines:

- *American Atheist: A Journal of Atheist News and Thought* (www.americanatheist.org)
- *Amsterdam News* (www.amsterdamnews.org/news/default.asp)
- *Asian Week* (news.asianweek.com/news)
- *Cineaste: Magazine on the Art and Politics of the Cinema* (www.cineaste.com)

- *ColorLines Magazine: Race, Culture and Action* (www.ctwo.org)
- *Extra! Fairness and Accuracy in Reporting* (www.fair.org/extra/index.htmlwww.fair.org/extra/index.html)
- *GeneWatch: A Bulletin for the Council for Responsible Genetics* (www.gene-watch.org)
- *In These Times* (www.inthesetimes.com)
- *Journal of Prisoners on Prisons* (www.jpp.org)
- *Monthly Review: An Independent Socialist Magazine* (www.monthlyreview.org)
- *Off Our Backs* (lesbian feminist politics) (www.offourbacks.org)
- *Texas Observer: A Journal of Free Voices* (texasobserver.org)

Examples of databases that specialize in alternative publications include the following:

- *Alternative Press Index*
- *Al-t PressWatch*
- *Chicano Database*
- *Ethnic NewsWatch*
- *Ethnic News (Lexis/Nexis)*
- *GenderWatch*[11]
- *Left Index*

Political Blogs   The freewheeling blogs (short for Web logs), otherwise known as online diaries, emerged out of distrust toward big media's incompetent journalists, homogeneity of news, and bypassing of ideas and stories. Bloggers post immediate personal reactions to commentary, events, and news reported in the mainstream press. Blogs are biased and proud of it. As *Time* points out, "Blogs don't pretend to be neutral: they're gleefully, unabashedly biased." Moreover, blogs "act like a lens, focusing attention on an issue until it catches fire."[12] For example, bloggers were the first to challenge the authenticity of the documents that CBS claimed proved George W. Bush received preferential treatment during his National Guard service.[13] Defenders of blogs praise them for opening up political and cultural discourse and challenging the credibility of the mainstream press. Critics, on the other hand, argue that bloggers are biased, insular, and operate outside the rules of journalism, ignoring objectivity, editing, and fact checking. Finally, while blogs offer fresh insights and at times serve as effective fact checkers to mainstream news services, they also spread gossip, unsubstantiated information, and spin. Thus, students must be instructed to apply the same skepticism to blogs as they would any other source of information.

Examples of political blogs include the following:

- instapundit.com
- littlegreenfootballs.com
- talkingpointsmemo.com
- www.andrewsullivan.com/index.php
- www.ojr.org/ojr/blog

Examples of blog search engines and directories include the following:

- Fagan Finder (www.faganfinder.com/blogs)
- Google Weblog Directory (blogsearch.google.com)
- Topix.net: Top Stories in Blogosphere (www.topix.net/blogs)
- Yahoo Weblog Directory (dir.yahoo.com)

The Popular Press in Academics, Citizenship, and Careers

Academics   Newspapers, magazines, and the trades lack scholarly status. Nonetheless, they can alert researchers to current and future trends. For example, an article in *Business Week* reports, "New studies point the way to more effective use of lung cancer drugs."[14] While lacking specific references, the student could use the alert to do a follow-up search on the increasing effectiveness of drugs used to treat lung cancer. The popular press also announces new releases of scholarly studies, reports, and surveys. For example, Roger Highfield reported in the *Daily Telegraph* that a new University of Michigan study has shown that "a lovey-dovey movie can put couples in a romantic mood."[15] Granted, some detective work is usually required to locate the exact study because most of these "research alerts" rarely provide full citations. While the popular media lacks the same level of authority and analysis as peer-reviewed journals, popular periodicals can fill gaps left by the scholarly press. Because the popular press is not bound by scholarly standards and the peer-review process, information can be disseminated much quicker. Thus, scanning relevant current popular print media for announcements of current research can be very advantageous.

Citizenship   In addition to keeping abreast of current research, reading newsweeklies can engender an awareness of national and world affairs. Consider September 11, 2001. Like many Americans, college students were not only shocked by the terrorist attacks on September 11 but also were blindsided; they could not fathom why Arab terrorists would want to attack America. Yet, perhaps students would not have been taken so unawares if they had been regular news readers of foreign affairs. If they had, their uncertainty as to what happened might have been mitigated. Regular news readers become better-informed citizens and voters. They become less reliant on friends and family for information and gain confidence in drawing their own conclusions based on sources.

Careers   Knowing what is going on in the world enhances one's conversational skills in the workplace. Having the confidence to converse on a myriad of topics reduces the fear of saying something stupid or being at a loss of what to say to the boss. Further, being a sophisticated conversationalist may give one an edge when interviewing for a job, negotiating a business deal, or forming a business relationship.

Scholarly Press

Scholarly Journals Are the Heavyweights in Academia.   Scholarly journals bring new contributions to knowledge and ensure the continuity of the literature in a research field. Three basic types of journals exist in most disciplines: research, theoretical, and applied/practical. Typically, the most prestigious journals are peer-reviewed, which means manuscripts undergo an intense examination by the editor and two or more reviewers who are unknown to the author (i.e., a blind review). However, a few highly respected journals (e.g., *Harvard Educational Review*) are nonrefereed, either because their prestigious status attracts top scholars or the editors want more control over journal content.[16]

Scholarly Journals Challenge Students.   Unlike pop magazines, scholarly journals terrify many students. They are intimidated by the technical content and unfamiliar with the methods of presentation and the jargon used to communicate information. Thus, to help mitigate students' trepidation of scholarly content, encourage them to skip the in-between material (i.e., the detailed data used to support the authors' theses or hypotheses) and concentrate on the understanding introduction and conclusion as well as deciphering the author's thesis or hypothesis. As students become familiar with reading about the subject in journals, they will begin to feel comfortable interpreting results and identifying strengths and weakness of the article. In the process, students will become increasingly confident in working with the evidence-based approach.

One caveat of emphasizing the importance of scholarly journals—many students will leave the classroom thinking that everything published in journals is true and anything written for the popular press is biased, false, or trivial. It is probably wise to emphasize the importance of scholarly journals but with the proviso that just because an article is published in a scholarly does not automatically make it authoritative or that it significantly contributes to the field.

General Types of Scholarly Articles Following are major types of scholarly articles:

- Research Reports: data from original empirical or scientific results; contributes to theory, concept analysis, research, or practice
- Practice: qualitative or quantitative assessment of methods, applications, strategies, and so on
- Technical Reports: significant advances of methods, practices, and techniques
- Literature Reviews: surveys of what is known about a topic. For example, these articles are reviews of literature:

  "Biological Influences on Homosexuality: Current Findings and Future"[17]
  "Tube Feeding in Patients with Advanced Dementia: A Review of the Evidence"[18]
  "The Concept of Popular Religion: A Literature Review."[19]

  Literature reviews can be very beneficial to a student's research. Reviews of research describe, compare, and contrast research in a subject area and evaluate the interpretation of thesis, argumentation, method, and evidence and the degree to which it contributes to the field. Many literature reviews will identify gaps and suggest future directions for research. Nearly all disciplines have journals that publish literature review articles as well as sources that are devoted to literature reviews, such as *Annual Review of Biochemistry*, *Annual Review of Sociology*, and *American Literary Scholarship*.[20]

Objective 3: Understand the Editorial Practices of Periodicals.

Editorial Perspectives   Magazines and scholarly journals differ radically in their purpose and content. Whereas journal articles vary in type, they all must substantiate a thesis or hypothesis through interpretation, observation, experiments, or theory. Conversely, popular media aim to inform, interpret, entertain, advocate, or teach. In theory, objectivity and balance are generally valued by most magazines and journals, however several factors can affect these values. In the case of magazines, objectivity can be influenced by advertisers, the parent company, or the sociopolitical orientation of the editorial staff. Objectivity in journals, on the other hand, can be colored by an editor's biases toward certain theoretical or methodological approaches or predispositions to an author because of institutional affiliations.[21]

Audiences   While academic and many popular magazines target specialized audiences, the audiences of the former are smaller and less diverse than the latter. A journal's audience is a tightly knit community composed of scholars, students, and instructors who are interested in deepening their knowledge of a very specific research area. Readers of magazines, on the other hand, read for a variety of reasons: they may want to be entertained, to relax, or to understand current events.

Acceptance and Rejection Practices   The review policies of journals differ from magazines in how they assess, accept, and reject articles. Unlike the scholarly press, the popular press does not have a rigorous review process. While journals depend, for the most part, on solicitations from scholars, many mass market magazines employ a staff of writers or hire freelancers or stringers to write stories from outlines suggested by the editor. Other magazines rely on unsolicited material, which is accepted or rejected by the editor based on audience and advertiser appeal.

Manuscripts submitted to a scholarly journal undergo a peer-review process. The manuscript is reviewed either by external reviewers or by selected members of the journal's editorial review board. In an external review, the editor sends an article to two or more referees who are identified as experts in the field. An alternative to the external review is one in which referees are selected from the journal's editorial review board. To ensure objectivity, the review process may be "blind," meaning the author's identity is unknown to the reviewers or "double blind" where the reviewers and author are unknown to each other. In either case, the reviewers evaluate the manuscript based on its significance to the field, methodological approach, and presentation. Each reviewer makes recommendations to the journal editor. Based on these comments, as well the editor's own reading, the fate of the manuscript may be as follows:

- The article is accepted as is.
- The article is conditionally accepted, provided the author agrees to make revisions.
- If there is a "tie" between the reviewers, the editor may invite the author to submit a rebuttal.
- The article is judged to be potentially publishable, and the author is invited to resubmit the article with improvements.
- The article is rejected outright because of faulty research, poor methodology, or sloppy writing.

The peer-review process is not entirely a "fraud detector."[22] Occasionally, manuscripts clear the peer-review process and are published, after which it is discovered that the authors used flawed or fabricated data. Referees are not always privy to the data and methods authors use to write their articles. In addition, reviewers may not devote the time required to scrutinize the data and scientific method. The peer-review process is based on trust; it is assumed that the research has been conducted according to standards of scholarship. However, some studies that have been successfully peer reviewed have been contradicted by subsequent research. In his 2005 study on flawed research, John Ioannidis of Tufts University School of Medicine, concludes that nearly "one-third of top research articles have been either contradicted or seriously questioned."[23]

In response to publicized reports of fraudulent and flawed research, many are debating the value of the peer review process. Peter Hernon and Candy Schwartz articulate some of these issues:

- Are [peer reviewers] accountable? To whom?
- Should the results of [peer] reviews remain confidential?
- Does peer review improve the quality of published research?[24]

While many journal editors believe the peer-review process is not "broken" and has been instrumental in "sav[ing] countless prominent scientists from publishing seriously flawed work," others in the scientific community feel peer review is "outdated and outmoded" and radical changes are required.[25] One change that has been suggested is to remove anonymity from the process and "replace [it with] a version of Amazon.com, in which scientists from around the world contribute their thoughts to constantly updated research."[26]

How can students determine whether a periodical is peer reviewed? Unfortunately, there is no one source that helps students determine which of the thousands of periodicals are peer reviewed. However, here are some tools and strategies that can assist them:

- Ulrich's *International Periodical Directory*
- Katz's *Magazines for Libraries*
- a journal's website links, such as "Submission Guidelines," "Editorial Policy," or "Notes to Contributors"
- the submission guidelines in the print versions of journals

Note: Be wary of trusting subscription databases to correctly tag those periodicals that are peer reviewed. For example, *The Humanist* is tagged as a peer-reviewed journal by *Academic Search Elite*.

CLASS ACTIVITIES

One-Hour Sessions

1. To develop students' ability to differentiate popular, trade, and scholarly periodicals, display examples of scholarly journals, preferably those that relate to the course content. Ask the class to mentally compare and contrast these journals with popular magazines that they have read. If there is time, solicit comments on the differences, and try to get students to tease out the most significant differences.

2. To reinforce a brief discussion on scholarly versus popular press, distribute a chart that illustrates the differences between the different types of periodicals. See later in this chapter, "Websites on Periodical Types."

3. For beginning students, give tips on how they can approach a scholarly article by first reading its introduction and conclusion and skipping the middle portions. To help students understand the jargon, remind them to consult the library's specialized dictionaries.

4. Show students how to limit database searches to peer-reviewed journals.

Multiple Sessions and Courses

1. To develop students' ability to differentiate between periodical types, display examples of popular, alternative, trade, and scholarly periodicals. Ask the class to compare and contrast them and identify at least three major differences between the four types.

   Today, news is disseminated in a variety of ways. Help students identify the different news outlets [e.g., newspapers, newsweeklies (print and electronic), blogs, RSS feeds, and personalized news services]. A good starting point is the tutorial "News Sources: An Overview," developed by Ohio State University Libraries (gateway. lib.ohio-state.edu/tutor/news).

2. Do some role-playing to help students understand how tabloid writers, journalists, and scholars gather information. For example:

   INSTRUCTOR: Pretend I am the editor of [name a tabloid]. I want you to write a juicy profile on [name a celebrity or politician]. Now, where and how are you going to get the "dirt" on this person?

   INSTRUCTOR: Pretend you are a journalist writing for [name a newspaper or magazine]. You have been assigned to write an investigative piece on [name a controversial topic]. What sources would you use? Who would you contact? What pictures would you use to tell the story? What background research is required?

INSTRUCTOR: Pretend you are a psychologist and you would like to study [name a topic]. How are you going to measure or assess this behavior? Will you use tests? Telephone surveys? Focus groups? Questionnaires?

3. Reinforce the fact that some subscription databases will index periodicals ranging from the popular to the scholarly. Examine the results of a search that covers a topic (e.g., personal ads) in both popular and scholarly articles. Discuss how each type of periodical treats the topic based on how titles are expressed and content is described in abstracts.

4. Illustrate the differences in points of view among newsmagazines. Use a controversial topic to discuss how conservative/libertarian, moderate, and liberal/progressive periodicals would frame the issue. The following list places mainstream newsmagazines within the political spectrum:

- Conservative/Libertarian
  American Spectator
  New Republic
  New American
- Moderate
  Time
  Newsweek
  U.S. News and World Report
- Liberal/Progressive
  Nation
  Progressive
  Mother Jones

Include in the discussion ways in which students can identify point of view. For example, political perspectives embed stock phrases. Karen Diaz and Nancy O'Hanlon identify several buzzwords for conservative/libertarian publications (e.g., *free enterprise, family values,* and *states' rights*) and liberal/progressive magazines (e.g., *equity, inclusion,* and *sustainable development*).[27]

5. To help students become familiar with alternative periodicals, ask them to compare the results of a search in an alternative press index with the results of a search in a general periodical index.

6. Emphasize the value of the author's works cited. To help students know the importance and benefits of the literature cited in an article, have them examine references from a scholarly article. Ask them to look at each reference and determine if it is a book, article, conference paper, government document, and so on. Then, focus on one citation and discuss how one would locate the full text of the item.

7. Provide an article in a popular magazine or newspaper that announces the release of a new study, and ask the students to try to find the full text. For example, the following is an excerpt from a *New York Times* article announcing the release of new evidence concerning early education:

> Now evidence from an experiment that has lasted nearly four decades may revive Horace Mann's faith. "Lifetime Effects: The High/Scope Perry Preschool Study Through Age 40" was released earlier this week. It shows that an innovative early education program can make a marked difference in the lives of poor minority youngsters—not just while they are in school but for decades afterward.[28]

Note that the article does not provide information on the exact location of the study. All we have is the title of the report. Ask the students how they would go about procuring the full text of the study. In this case, the full report can be found by entering the title of the study as a Google search, which points to the High Scope Educational Research Foundation (www.highscope.org/Research/PerryProject/perrymain.htm).

To develop other examples from newspapers or magazines, enter a search with the keyword *study* and connect it to a topic in Lexis/Nexis or a general periodical database. For example:

study
AND
(preschool OR early education OR head start)

8. To help students understand the parts of a scientific article use the following resources:

- Ann McNeal, "How to Read a Scientific Research Paper: A Four-Step Guide for Students and Faculty," helios.hampshire. edu/~apmNS/design/RESOURCES/HOW_READ.html.
- M. Purugganan and J. Hewitt, "How to Read a Scientific Paper" (2004), www.owlnet.rice.edu/~cainproj/courses/sci_article. doc. Includes a template to guide students in taking notes on research articles.

INSTRUCTOR GUIDES, HANDOUTS, AND EXERCISES

Websites on Periodical Types

Following are charts that distinguish between the popular, trade, and scholarly presses.

1. Austin Community College Library, "What's the Difference: Popular Magazine, Science Magazine, Journal" (January 12, 2004), library.austincc.edu/help/chem1411/magjnl.htm. This site focuses on comparisons to science periodicals.
2. California State University, Northridge, "Types of Periodicals" (September 28, 2000), library.csun.edu/mwoodley/Scholarly. html.
3. Cornell University, Africana Library, "Types of Periodicals" (July 2, 2002), www.library.cornell.edu/africana/guides/periodicals.htm.
4. Harvard College Library, "Popular Magazines and Scholarly Journals: Characteristics and Differences" (August 18, 2006), hcl. harvard.edu/research/guides/lamont_handouts/scholarlyjournals. html. Accompanying the chart is an annotated listed of cultural and intellectual magazines.
5. Ohio State University Library, "Types of Articles" (2004), gateway.lib.ohio-state.edu/tutor/articles/pg1.html.

6. Rutgers University Libraries, "Scholarly Peer-Reviewed Literature vs. Popular Literature: What's the Difference?" (April 26, 2005), www.libraries.rutgers.edu/rul/indexes/scholarly_articles.shtml.

7. Skyline College Library, "Types of Periodicals," smccd.net/accounts/skylib/lsci100/lesson6_2.htm.

8. University of Maryland Libraries, "Identifying Periodical Types" (2006), www.lib.umd.edu/guides/journals.html.

9. University of Oregon Libraries, "Types of Periodicals" (September 22, 2006), libweb.uoregon.edu/guides/findarticles/distinguish.html.

10. University of Texas, Permian Basin Library, "Types of Periodicals" (August 21, 2006), www.utpb.edu/library/sertypes.html. Provides a detailed breakdown of periodicals of opinion, policy and influence, and research and scholarship.

Assessment Tools

1. Compare and contrast the differences between popular and scholarly discussions of a social issue, historical event, or scientific topic. Students can compare how each source frames the topic, how it supports its argument with statements and conclusions, and how it documents its sources. The articles can be supplied by the instructor or the student can be responsible for finding the articles. The latter will give students experience in using periodical databases.

2. Ask students to evaluate a scholarly article. Some of the criteria may include:

- What are the author's credentials? Do they pertain to the topic of the article?
- Who is the targeted audience (laypeople, policymakers, practitioners, researchers, etc.)?
- What is the author's point of view? Does he or she state any biases?
- What method was used to get the data (anecdotal, opinion/experience, interviews, original research, questionnaires, lab/field experiments, empirical, etc.)?
- Does the author clearly state conclusions or imply them?

- Are the conclusions based on sound logic and outside evidence? Or are they skewed by bias?
- Does the study fly in the face of established research, policy, or theory?
- Are there other studies that support the conclusions of this article?[29]

The following are resources that describe specific teaching strategies:

1. James E. Bird, "Teaching from the Journal: An Instructional Method," *Research Strategies* 15, no. 4 (1997): 293–300. Demonstrates how to teach upper-division science students the peer-review process and how to read parts of a journal including author(s), abstract, keywords, and acknowledgements.
2. Mark McKnight, "Introduction to Research in Music" (June 21, 2004), www.library.unt.edu/music/classes/mumh5410/assign8.htm. A four-part assignment in which students: (1) respond to a series of questions based on the *periodicals* entry in the *New Grove Dictionary* (2) identify five periodicals that relate to the students' area of interest (3) research music indexes and (4) locate and annotate ten sources on a topic of the student's choice.
3. K. Murphy and S. Turaba, "Queer Periodicals Assignment," www.wesleyan.edu/libr/schome/exhibit/Teaching/Pedagogy/queer.doc. Students are given a set of criteria in which they are to "document" a periodical. While focusing on periodicals on homosexuality, this assignment can be adapted to any discipline or subject.
4. Janet S. Russell, Lucy Martin, and Dara Curtin, "Non-science Majors Gain Valuable Insight Studying Clinical Trials Literature: An Evidence-Based Medicine Library Assignment," *Advances in Physiology Education* 28 (2004): 188–94. The science librarian and instructor collaborate on an assignment that requires students to research a medical condition. They are to research primary and secondary sources. The final project is a poster presentation.

Tutorials and Quizzes

The following are tutorials and quizzes on periodical basics:

1. American University Library, "Periodicals Tutorial and Quiz" (December 12, 2004), www.library.american.edu/tutorial/type7.html. Multiple-choice quiz on correctly identifying periodical types.
2. Duke University Libraries, "Finding Review Articles," www.lib. duke.edu/libguide/fi_review.htm. Graphic tutorial on locating review literature.
3. East Carolina University, Joyner Library, "Periodicals: Scholarly, Popular, Trade?" (December 29, 2005), www.ecu.edu/cs-lib/reference/compare.cfm. Provides a brief quiz on identifying scholarly periodicals.
4. Glendale College Library, "Differences between Magazines and Journals," www.glendale.edu/library/instruction/LibWorkshops/ ImprovLibResHandout.pdf. Provides an assignment on differentiating popular and scholarly periodicals.
5. Gail Gradowski and Monica Smith, Santa Clara University Library, www.scu.edu/library/services/reference/is/tutorials/periodicals/mod1/partonepage1.html. Tutorial includes a detailed graphic discussion on scholarly journals.
6. IUPUI University Library, "Inflite: Information Literacy Tutorial," (2002) inflite.ulib.iupui.edu.
7. Iowa State University, "Evaluating Books' and Journal Articles' Information," www.lib.iastate.edu/commons/old_resources/printeval. Provides a set of questions for evaluating books and articles, covering authorship, publisher, peer review, purpose, and usefulness.
8. Long Beach City College Library, "Evaluating Information," lib. lbcc.edu/class2/quiz4.pdf. Provides an assignment that makes comparisons between types of periodicals.
10. Ohio State University, "Tutorial: Finding Periodicals" (March 14, 2002), gateway.lib.ohio-state.edu/tutor/articles/index.html. Tutorial includes a graphic explanation of the components of a scholarly article. Brief quiz included.
11. Oregon State University Library, "Evaluating Periodical Articles" (September 12, 2003), osulibrary.oregonstate.edu/instruction/tutorials/refine/articles. Tutorial on evaluating periodicals, focusing on audience, type, and content.
12. Santa Clara University, Library, "Finding Scholarly Periodicals: Module 1: Types of Periodicals" (November 8, 2006), www.scu.

edu/library/services/reference/is/tutorials/periodicals/index.html.
Detailed graphic tutorial on the different types of periodicals.

13. Skyline College Library, "Lesson Six: Periodical Literature,"
smccd.net/accounts/skylib/ lsci100/lesson6_ex.htm. Includes an
interactive quiz on the types of periodicals, their differences with
other types of literature, and choosing appropriate databases.

14. University of Mary Washington, "Talon Module 6: Finding Periodical Articles," www.library.umw.edu/talon/periodicals.html.
Tutorial ranges from definitions and types of periodicals to locating them in online databases.

15. University of Massachusetts, Boston Library, "Topics and Types
of Periodicals" (2001), www.lib.umb.edu/webtutorial/module7/
Module7-6a.html. Multiple-choice quiz on matching topic to appropriate periodical type.

16. University of North Carolina, Chapel Hill, Library, "Evaluating
Articles" (2004), www.lib.unc.edu/instruct/evaluate. Provides a
tutorial and quiz.

17. University of Texas System Digital Library, "Tilt: Interactive Library Tutorial" (2004), tilt.lib.utsystem.edu.

18. Western Michigan University Library, "SearchPath: A Library
Tutorial" (2002), www.wmich.edu/library/searchpath.

NOTES

1. *Oxford English Dictionary*, 1989 ed., s.v. "periodical."

2. For additional listings of regional, national, and international newspapers,
go to Yahoo! News Directory at dir.yahoo.com/News_and_Media/Newspapers.

3. Russell Lynes, "Highbrow, Lowbrow, Middlebrow," *Harper's Magazine*,
February 1949, 19–28.

4. For a full treatment of periodical databases, see chapter 5.

5. "Time's 25 Most Influential Americans," *Time*, April 1997, 149.

6. Jim Hogshire, *Grossed-Out Surgeon Vomits inside Patient: An Insider's
Look at Supermarket Tabloids* (Venice, CA: Feral House, 1997), 7.

7. Bill Kovah and Tom Rosenstiel, *Warp Speed: America in the Age of
Mixed Media* (New York: Century Foundation, 1999), 4.

8. For a list of additional tabloid magazines, go to Yahoo! Directory at dir.
yahoo.com/Entertainment/News_and_Media/Magazines/Tabloids.

9. Carl Jensen and Peter Phillips, *Project Censored: 2003* (Chapel Hill, NC: Shelburne, 2004), 51–53.

10. Thomas J. Nagy. "The Secret behind the Sanctions: How the U.S. Intentionally Destroyed Iraq's Water Supply," *The Progressive*, September 2001, 22–25.

11. For lists of alternative publications, go to Alternative Press Center's Online Directory at www.altpress.org/direct.html and Yahoo News Directory at dir.yahoo.com/News_and_Media/Newspapers/Alternative_Newsweeklies.

12. Lev Grossman, et al., "Meet Joe Blog," *Time*, June 21, 2004, 66.

13. The authenticity of the documents in question remains inconclusive; however, an independent investigation did find that the developers of the story failed to follow sound journalistic principles. See "CBS Dismisses Four over Broadcast on Bush Service," *New York Times*, January 11, 2005, A1.

14. Catherine Arnst, "Taking Better Aim at Cancer," *Business Week*, May 2004, 108.

15. Roger Highfield, "Weepie or Action Movie? It's in the Hormones, Says Study," *Daily Telegraph*, July 28, 2004, voyager.lib.csub.edu:2070/universe/document.

16. Kenneth Henson, "Writing for Professional Journals: Paradoxes and Promises," *Phi Delta Kappan*, June 2001, 767.

17. Joel E. Alexander, "Biological Influences on Homosexuality: Current Findings and Future Directions," *Psychology, Evolution and Gender* 2 (2000): 241–52.

18. T. E. Finucane, "Tube Feeding in Patients with Advanced Dementia: A Review of the Evidence," *JAMA: Journal of the American Medical Association* 282 (1999): 1365.

19. Maria Teresa Dawson, "The Concept of Popular Religion: A Literature Review," *Journal of Iberian and Latin American Studies* 7, no. 1 (2001): 105–32.

20. For a clear PowerPoint presentation on literature reviews, see Ann Nolan and Dawn Wright, "Literature Reviews: The Hows, Whys, and Wherefores," dusk.geo.orst.edu/prosem/Week2PPT.

21. Joann Miller and Robert Perrucci, "Back Stage at Social Problems: An Analysis of the Editorial Decision Process, 1993–1996" *Social Problems* 48, no. 1 (2001): 93–110.

22. Anna Fazackerley, "Review by Peers 'Good For Science,'" *Times Higher Education Supplement*, June 25, 2004, 5.

23. As reported in Michael Kranish, "Flaws Are Found in Validating Medical Studies: Many See Need to Overhaul Standards for Peer Review," *Boston Globe*, August 15, 2005, A1. The citation for J. P. Ioannidis's study is: "Contra-

dicted and Initially Stronger Effects in Highly Cited Clinical Research," *JAMA: Journal of the American Medical Association*, 294 (2005): 218–28.

24. Peter Hernon and Candy Schwartz, "Peer Review Revisited: An Editorial," *Library and Information Science Research* 28 (2006): 2.

25. Kranish, "Flaws Are Found."

26. Kranish, "Flaws Are Found."

27. Karen Diaz and Nancy O'Hanlon, *IssueWeb: A Guide and Sourcebook for Researching Controversial Issues on the Web*, (Westport, CT: Libraries Unlimited, 2004).

28. David L. Kirp, "Life Way after Head Start," *New York Times*, sec. 6, November 21, 2004.

29. For an expanded version of this assignment, see Eugene A. Engeldinger and Beverly Pestel, "Location and Evaluation of Chemistry Literature," *Research Strategies* 9, no. 3 (Summer 1991): 142–46. For additional guides to evaluating an empirical article, go to University of Texas Houston, Health Center, "Guidelines for Literature Reviews," blue.utb.edu/sfisherhoch/Projects/literaturereview.htm.

5

SEARCH STRATEGIES FOR
PERIODICAL DATABASES

Goal: To recognize electronic periodical databases and demonstrate how to search them for relevant documents.
Objective 1: Define a periodical database and identify the major types.
Objective 2: Choose an appropriate database.
Objective 3: Know the organization of periodical databases.
Objective 4: Perform basic search strategies in periodical databases.

In the old days, students hoped to find articles either by flipping through stacks of periodicals or looking through a mountain of print indexes and were often disappointed with the results of their searches. Nowadays, due to the speed and ease of electronic databases, access is easier, and, as a result, students often have unrealistic expectations of what these databases can deliver. Students demand a lot: they want *their* periodicals fully indexed with deep backfiles and, of course, with full text. Unfortunately these high expectations cannot always be met because database providers may

- selectively index, which means certain articles and reviews never make it into the database;
- restrict years of coverage; or
- fail to provide full text.

The access status of the core journal *Historian* is a good example of the unpredictability of access. No one database offers complete indexing and full text coverage of this journal, which began publication in 1938. While several database providers include this journal, their coverage varies, and none offer indexing or back files before the 1990s, except for CLIO's *Historical Abstracts* and *America: History* and *Life*, which index *Historian* back to the mid-1950s. Thus, the only way to access references in *Historian* from 1938 to the early 1950s is to consult print sources such as *Combined Retrospective Index to Journals in History, 1838-1974*. Moreover, there is no full-text access from *Historian's* inception through the 1980s. Luckily, however, the publisher has not embargoed this title, but delivery of the full-text content has been delayed for a period of time. For many periodicals, especially journals, publishers delay availability of issues anywhere from a week to more than a year.

Many students expect "one-stop shopping" when searching a database. They assume that one database will supply all the articles they need for a project. Unfortunately, all-inclusiveness is too expensive for database publishers. Thus, the titles providers include are influenced by such factors as editorial content, timeliness, scholarly conventions, peer review, citation data, and diversity of authors. Providers are especially vigilant when adding e-journals, as Web publishing is easy and inexpensive, and many publications only appear to be scholarly. As Craig Emerson and Michael Miyazaki observe, "Web journals have the look and feel of cutting-edge research, but they have little or no peer review."[1]

Databases intimidate novice users with their complex functions; therfore, many indulge in a kind of magical thinking about their capabilities. These users believe that databases are all-knowing and that entering a few keywords will retrieve what is needed. But as experienced searchers know, computers are quite stupid. For example, while a user enters the word *dove* intending it mean the bird, his or her search set will be littered with other meanings of the word, such as:

- the past tense of *dive*,
- the poet Rita Dove,
- a surname for an author,
- a political label for a person opposite a hawk,
- the brand name for the ice cream product, and

• the brand name for skin- and hair-care products

Computers process words not as meaningful objects but simply as letters strung together. Thus, the search results are only as good as the user is at formulating search strategies. Another kind of magical thinking that students indulge in is that by entering one or two words to describe their topic, the computer will "know" what they want. For example, by entering *guns*, they assume the database will also retrieve articles on

• handguns,
• assault weapons,
• shotguns,
• semiautomatics,
• rifles,
• firearms, and
• revolvers

In the minds of the students, *guns* is an umbrella term, and the computer will know this and consequently pull all articles that deal with any type of gun.

Students lose this magical thinking when they begin to learn and practice searching skills. They learn that the computer is simply a tool that needs a human to tell it exactly what to do in order for relevant hits to appear. The challenge for the instructor is to teach the conceptual and mechanical skills necessary to perform successful searches in the time allotted for the library session(s). No student grasps intricate searching skills immediately. Successful searching requires substantial experience in conducting searches, reflecting on the success of each search, and modifying the search to boost the rate of relevancy in retrievals.

LEARNING OBJECTIVES AND INSTRUCTOR ACTIVITIES

Objective 1: Define a Periodical Database and Identify the Major Types.

Prior to building a successful search query, few students, other than perhaps computer science majors, need to know the intricacies of databases; they just need to know the basics: what they are, the major types, and their contents. The following outlines the basics of electronic periodical databases.

What Is an Electronic Periodical Database?   A periodical database is classed as a bibliographical database, which is a collection of published material entered, stored, and delivered via an aggregator, commercial vendor, CD-ROM, or online public access catalog (OPAC). Periodical databases contain references to newspapers, magazines, and journals but often contain other material such as book chapters, conference papers, and dissertations. Other bibliographic databases include OPACs, reference material (e.g., *Dictionary of Literary Biography*), and directories (e.g., *Foundation Directory Online*).

How Are Periodical Databases Categorized?   There are four types of periodical databases:

1. citation—provides only references, often with abstracts
2. full text—contains references, often with abstracts, and are accompanied with full text or links to a full-text version indexed in another database or aggregator
3. hybrid—provides citations, often with abstracts, some of which may be accompanied by full text or links to full text
4. citators—provides citations, often with abstracts, and cited references.

The type of periodicals varies among databases: some restrict content to scholarly material; others include only magazines and newspapers; while still others combine the professional and the popular. Some databases supplement periodical literature with other resources, such as dissertations, books, book chapters, essays, government documents, conference proceedings, and websites.

What Are Multidisciplinary and Specialized Databases?   The multidisciplinary databases, such as *Academic Search Elite*, form the nucleus of a library's core database collection. Supplementing the multidisciplinary databases are the specialized databases that emphasize a particular subject or discipline. A library's collection of specialized databases reflects the focus of the academic curriculum. Table 5.1 lists examples of multidisciplinary and specialized databases. Whether multidisciplinary

Table 5.1. Multidisciplinary and Specialized Databases

Multidisciplinary	Specialized
Academic Search Premier	PsycInfo
Expanded Academic ASAP	Sociological Abstracts
ProQuest Research Library	Biosis
WilsonWeb	MLA International Bibliography

or specialized, no one periodical database can guarantee complete coverage of a topic. Students should be encouraged to identify and search several databases that most likely will have material on their topic.

Objective 2: Choose an Appropriate Database.

Part of a successful research strategy is targeting the right databases to search. To help students identify the appropriate databases, ask them to consider these factors:

1. Know when to use a periodical database. Often students who need a specific answer to a question will go to periodical databases when they probably need to go to a reference/directory database.
2. Become familiar with the library's databases. Make a list of those that most likely will provide relevant articles. When in doubt consult a mulitdisciplinary database first.
3. Determine the coverage of the database. How current is it? How far back does it go?
4. Know the level of detail covered in the database. Does the database focus on material that is overly detailed or technical? For example, while *Medline* is a major database for diabetes articles, its technical language would be inappropriate for English composition students researching the causes of diabetes. They should start with a general periodical database, such as *Academic Search Elite*.

Objective 3: Know the Organization of Periodical Databases.

The thousands of article citations stored in a periodical database are useless unless the database program facilitates access and dissemination. Without such a program, looking for articles on a topic would be akin to trying to find a specific record in a warehouse where thousands of records are shelved willy-nilly. At the risk of oversimplifying, a database management program creates order by constructing an index from all words and phrases embedded in the records with the exception of stopwords, that is, common words such as *a*, *the*, and *of*). Alongside each indexed word, the number of records that include that word or phrase is noted. For example, table 5.2 illustrates a portion of an index from a hypothetical periodical database. As shown, *formaldehyde* appears in 108 records, clearly not as popular as the word *form*, which is embedded in 15,995 records. The words in the index are pulled from the records stored in the database. Each record represents a document. Data about that document is broken up into "fields." Each field contains a piece of information about the article.

The generic record in table 5.3 illustrates basic, searchable fields that most periodical databases include: author, title, source data, subject headings, and abstracts. Many specialized databases will often include searchable fields unique to its subject or discipline. For example, business databases will include searchable fields for industry codes and product names.

Table 5.2. Hypothetical Periodical Database Index

Words from Records	Number of Records
form	15,995
form letters	20
formaldehyde	108
formalism	537
formalists	274
forman, clyde	2
formation	5,009
former	13,076
former soviet republics	63

Table 5.3. Primary Searchable Fields in Periodical Databases

Field	Purpose
Title	title of periodical article
Authors	individuals who wrote article
Source	title of periodical
Document type	type of source (e.g., newspaper)
Subject headings	controlled vocabulary terms
Abstract	summary of article

The importance of fields extends beyond giving information about a document; they are integral to building an effective search strategy. Searching multiple fields may retrieve a high percentage of irrelevant hits, while searching one field will retrieve only a few or no hits. Novice students unwittingly rely on the "default" search, unaware of how fields can affect their searches and thus databases. Students need to know what the "default" search box is, what it includes, and the ramifications of searching it. Understanding field searching will enable students to better define, narrow, or limit a search.

The interfaces of many databases default to a "keyword" search box until it is overridden by the user. Depending upon the interface, the "default" field may do a keyword search of a combination of title, author, source, abstract, descriptor, and identifier fields. This inclusion of several fields can be advantageous for some topics, especially new phenomena and the esoteric, topics for which little has been written about. While, the default field can ferret out the new and unusual, it can skew relevancy for other types of topics by retrieving a high number of irrelevant records. Generally, the topics affected are those that have been widely discussed or contain familiar keywords. For example, consider the search strategy below on tobacco use among African Americans (truncation is ignored).

blacks OR African Americans
AND
tobacco OR cigarettes OR smoking OR nicotine

When this strategy is entered into a "default" field, the search set will result in scores of records, many of which will be only tangentially relevant or not relevant at all. However, when the search is limited to the "title" field, the results are far fewer yet most address the topic. Unrelated records are caught up in the results because keywords are searched in nontopical fields, such as the author field. For example, the truncated keyword "black*" will retrieve writers on tobacco use with surnames such as "Martin Black" or "Gillian Blackmore."

Equally important to search relevancy is the field limiter common on many interfaces. Basic field limiters allow the users to narrow their searches to

- document type,
- peer review,
- language,
- specific date ranges, and
- full text.

In addition, discipline-specific field limiters are featured on many specialized databases. For example, *PsycInfo* allows the user to restrict a search strategy to clinical trials while *CINAHL* offers a field limiting searches to outpatients.

Clearly, searchable fields and field limiters can be very effective in building a search strategy. Successful field searching depends upon users identifying fields appropriate for a particular topic. Generally, the user must experiment with different fields to determine which ones yield the best results.

Objective 4: Perform Basic Search Strategies in Periodical Databases.

Despite "user-friendly" databases and search engines, users still have problems searching. As mentioned earlier, naive students' expectations are high when searching, thus they are often disappointed when the search results contain no hits, too many hits, or no relevant hits. To help students become shrewd searchers, they should be taught

- the three basic techniques of configuring a subject query: Boolean (fully discussed in chapter 3), controlled vocabulary, and free text;
- the unique roles each of these techniques has in searching; and
- the situations in which to use each search technique.

While Boolean is the most sophisticated strategy to use when multiple variables or concepts is required, it is not always the best choice, and, in some cases, it can unnecessarily complicate a search. This is especially true for new concepts, esoteric topics, or names of relatively unknown individuals, theories, events, or organizations. For example, a complex search strategy is unnecessary when searching for Earthjustice, a non-profit law firm that handles environmental cases. All that is needed is to simply enter *Earthjustice*. There is no need to connect it (AND) with *law* or *environment* because few articles discuss this organization and doing so may even drop some hits. However, it is ill-advised to apply this simple keyword search when searching for articles on such groups as the Sierra Club. Its national prominence guarantees that hundreds of articles would be retrieved. Thus, to increase precision, the searcher would do well to connect Sierra Club with another topic—for example Sierra Club's position on immigration:

> Sierra Club
> AND
> immigration OR emigration OR migration

This refined search performed in a multidisciplinary database resulted in a core of thirty pertinent documents. Experience and skill teaches students which research situations demand one technique over another.

Controlled Vocabulary Humans use natural language to communicate with one another. Thus, for inexperienced searchers, it is natural for them to translate their topic to the computer using commonplace language. Unfortunately, computers do not understand natural language. For example, novice users are often surprised when they enter a word that happens to be a homograph, that is, words that are spelled the same but have different meanings (e.g., the word *draft*). A search retrieves records dealing with all meanings of the word, not just the one intended by the user.

Likewise, naive students often assume that their natural language query is a "catch-all," an umbrella term that will retrieve all records germane to their topic. But, of course, the computer does no such thing; it only retrieves records that use the combination of words expressed in the search string the user entered. For example, the string *teen dads* used as query will retrieve only those articles that have the combination *teen* and *dads* embedded in their records. But, what about those articles whose authors use other phrases to express the same issue? The following are other possible combinations:

- teenage fathers
- teen fathers
- young fathers

- teenage fatherhood
- adolescent fathers
- fathers in adolescence

Based on these combinations, *teen dads* is too restrictive of a search and would miss many relevant articles. As experienced searchers know, natural language often contains a variety words and phrases that express the same concept.

Clearly, there are myriad ways to express *teen dads*. Searched individually, each one of the above keyword phrases retrieves *some* articles, but many records will be overlooked. Therefore, to corral these various phrases that refer to the same concept, each record is assigned a single term to represent the various expressions of *teen dads*, so the searcher will retrieve all records that focus on that concept regardless of how it is expressed. For example, records dealing with teen dads are assigned the term *teenage fathers* in *Academic Search Elite* and *WilsonWeb's Omni-File*. However, while subject headings are standardized within a database, they are not standardized across databases. For instance, in *PsycInfo* and *Sociological Abstracts*, the more formal term *adolescent fathers* is used.

These standardized terms—also known as subject headings, preferred terms, descriptors, and, in the aggregate, a controlled vocabulary—are predetermined words or phrases that represent

- concepts,
- theories,
- individuals,
- population groups,
- social phenomena,
- activities, and
- events.

Probably the most famous example of controlled vocabulary is the yellow pages found in a city telephone directory. If one wants a list of hairdressers or hair stylists, chances are they will not be found under those headings but under something more formal and inclusive such as "Beauty Shops and Services." Controlled vocabularies serve to bring together similar documents and to clarify ambiguity. For example, the word *aids* can refer to teaching aids, hearing aids, and the disease Acquired Immune Deficiency Syndrome, otherwise known as AIDS. To separate the latter from the former terms, all documents that deal with the disease are grouped under the subject heading that might be labeled AIDS (Disease).

To help users use subject headings, some database publishers provide an online or print thesaurus. Some of the best known thesauri include *PsycInfo, Medical Subject Headings (MeSH)*, and *Education Resources Information Center (ERIC)*. Generally, thesauri

- identify controlled vocabulary terms;
- provide, via scope notes, definitions and parameters of terms; and
- suggest alternative terms synonyms.

Finally, many thesauri organize terms conceptually. Terms may be viewed hierarchically by being classed as broader or narrower. For example, *PsycInfo* lists the term *acculturation* as a narrower term for the broader term *cultural change*. Moreover, terms may display other terms associatively, meaning that terms can be linked to related terms and "see also" references. For example, a related term for *cultural change* is *modernization*. Hierarchial and associative terms are especially useful in identifying key synonyms for a specific concept. For example, a search strategy using the word *men* should include the synonym *males* and, if relevant, the narrower term *sons*. An associative term would be *masculinity*. Students should be taught the advantages of using thesauri, which can increase the number of relevant records as well enable the user to understand the semantic relationships that define a descriptor through scope notes and broader, narrower, and related terms.

Free-Text Searching Controlled vocabulary language can be a very powerful search aid, but it has its weaknesses, especially when the user is researching the arcane, the unusual, or something very specific. These topics often are not assigned descriptors, as they lack a substantial body of literature. Likewise, new phenomena are rarely assigned descriptors because creators of controlled vocabularies recognize that fads and the latest trends often disappear after having their "fifteen minutes of fame." However, a few fads and provocative phenomena persist and eventually become mainstream after being widely observed and studied. As Carolyn Heilbrun says, "Today's shocks are tomorrow's conventions."[2] And those "conventions" often end up as terms in a controlled vocabulary list. Nevertheless, controlled vocabulary lacks currency; there is a lag between the time the natural language enters into the controlled vocabulary.

To search the arcane, the unusual, and the latest fads effectively, searchers should use words from everyday speech, that is, words not included in controlled vocabularies. This search technique is referred to as natural language or free-text searching. For example, the South Beach Diet has been a wildly popular method of losing weight and has generated a lot of hype in the media since spring 2003. Yet, as of this writing, the *Academic Search Elite* thesaurus has no exclusive descriptor for the South Beach Diet. The closest matches in the controlled vocabulary list are *weight loss*, *reducing diets*, and *low carbohydrate diet*. Searching for articles devoted to the South Beach Diet under any one of these headings would be excruciatingly slow because the majority of the references will deal with diets other than South Beach. Therefore, simply entering *south beach diet* as a free-text search cuts through this tediousness and retrieves articles that focus on this diet.

In addition to new phenomena, free-text searching works best in two other research situations. First, when students know so little about the topic, they are confounded as to how to frame a query. To help students get started, have them enter colloquial expressions (e.g., slang and idioms) and study the subsequent results for relevant descriptors, better keywords, and synonyms to build a more effective search strategy. This way, they can begin to understand the words and phrases professional writers use to express a topic. For example, if *drunks* is entered in *Academic Search Elite*, several records will list *alcoholism* as the descriptor, while writers will include the term *alcoholics*. Hence, students can use those words to bring precision to their search strategy. Following is a brief list of informal words students often use to describe a concept, along with terms used by professional writers and found in controlled vocabularies:

- cars: automobiles, vehicles
- fat: overweight, obese
- hookers: prostitution, sex workers
- bums: street people, homeless, transients

- ads: advertisements, advertising, commercials
- unfaithful: adultery, infidelity, extramarital affairs
- cold turkey: detoxification, smoking cessation

Also, free-text searches are usually necessary when the topic is extremely specific or esoteric because these phenomena rarely have their own descriptors. Following is a selected list of what could be construed as very specific or esoteric:

- persons of minor importance in history
- minor theorists, practitioners, scientists
- lesser-known theories, applications, practices
- tests or measurements
- rare diseases
- minor organizations, societies, associations, and so on

Students should be taught that no one search technique is applicable to all search situations. This is true not only for periodical databases but also for OPACs and the Web. The nature of the topic dictates whether free text, controlled vocabulary, or Boolean is used. Or, in many cases, a topic might command that a combination of all three techniques be used.

Precision and Recall   Whatever the search method used, for a successful search, searchers need to decide what they expect from the resulting set of documents: high precision, high recall, or a balance of the two. Precision and recall measure the effectiveness of search results. High precision aims at a core of highly relevant hits but at the risk of dropping potentially useful articles. Search techniques that aim for high precision include:

- the use of several Boolean AND operators;
- the use of very narrow terms, for example, *obesogenic*; and
- the restriction of a search strategy to specific fields, such as the title field.

On the other hand, search techniques that aim for high recall retrieve lots of relevant documents but may include many irrelevant items. Search techniques that aim for high recall include:

- the use of several Boolean OR operators;
- a free-text search in multiple fields, for example, title, abstract, descriptor, and full text; and
- the use of broad descriptors or free-text words, for example, *environment*, *global*, and *achievement*.

A balance between high recall and high precision may be achieved by a well-constructed Boolean strategy or by building a search relying on descriptors from a well-constructed controlled vocabulary list.

To help users access subject headings, some database publishers provide an online or print thesaurus. The best of these thesauri

- identify controlled vocabulary terms;
- provide, via scope notes, definitions and parameters of terms; and
- suggest alternate terms or synonyms.

Many thesauri organize terms hierarchically, which can provide guidance in developing a search strategy. Students can browse the thesaurus, select a heading, and either search the articles assigned to the heading or zero in on the heading's narrower or related terms.

CLASS ACTIVITIES

The following strategies and activities stress the importance of approaching search strategies conceptually rather than haphazardly. Additional activities and assessments can be found in chapter 3.

One-Hour Sessions

Granted, teaching a full complement of search strategy methods is impossible during a one-shot session. However, it is possible to cover some aspects of free text, controlled vocabulary, and Boolean. Consider adapting the following instructional strategy that incorporates these three basic search techniques.

1. Pretend you are interested in writing about people who drink too much and you enter the topic phrase in *WilsonWeb's OmniFile*.

The search results in zero hits. So you modify the search and enter the colloquial word *drunks* (truncated "drunk*").

2. Scroll down the results list and find a title that looks interesting, such as "Social and Neighborhood Correlates of Adolescents Drunkenness: A Pilot Study in Cape Town, South Africa."

3. Click on it. After reading the abstract, you decide to focus on teens and alcohol without the South African perspective, so you peruse the subject headings and click on "Youth/Alcohol Use."

4. The results will be articles that focus only on youth and alcohol use. Examine them until you find one that looks promising, such as "A Longitudinal Study of the Relationship between Depressive Symptoms and Alcohol Use in a Sample of Inner-City Black Youth."

5. This article narrows the topic to teens, drinking, and depression.

6. Study the record's title, abstract, and subject headings and identify words that express your major concepts: *drunkenness*, *teens*, and *depression*. For example:

> Title: A Longitudinal Study of the Relationship between Depressive Symptoms and Alcohol Use in a Sample of Inner-City Black Youth. Author: Repetto, Paula B.; Zimmerman, Marc A.; Caldwell, Cleopatra H. Journal Name: Journal of Studies on Alcohol Source: Journal of Studies on Alcohol v. 65 no. 2 (March 2004) pp. 169–78.
>
> Abstract: Objective: the purpose of this study was to examine longitudinally the relationship between depressive symptoms and alcohol use in a sample of black youth. Method: participants were 458 black males and females interviewed annually during the high school years and then for 3 years during the transition to adulthood. The relationship was examined using growth curves with Hierarchical Linear Modeling.
>
> Subject(s): Teenagers/Alcohol use; Alcohol/Psychological aspects; Black youth/Psychology; Youth/Alcohol use; Mental depression; Drinking of alcoholic beverages/Psychological aspects; Depression in adolescence.[3]

7. Now let's build a search strategy that will be precise enough to retrieve a core of highly relevant articles. For example:

> (alcohol* OR drunk* OR drink*) AND (teen* OR high school* OR adolesc*) AND (depression OR depressive*)

8. (The instructor then plugs in the search strategy, and together, she and the students discuss the results.)

9. Okay, we retrieved some articles. At this point you either can collect these articles and read them or you may want to continue to check the library's list of databases and target at least two other databases that may also contain articles germane to our topic.

Following the above demonstration, and if workstations are available, have students practice searching their own topics. The goal of the activity should be that by the end of the session, students should have one or two relevant articles. If possible, pass out search strategy worksheets to help students design their research strategies. For a sample worksheet, see example 5.2. If there are not workstations, conduct one or two more demonstrations based on student suggestions.

Multiple Sessions and Courses

1. Over the course of several sessions, conduct search strategy demonstrations (like the one for a single session), each progressing in complexity. Reinforce the use of free text, controlled vocabulary, Boolean, truncation, and field limiters. The more students are exposed to and experience database searching, the better they get at building effective strategies.

2. To help students determine which databases will most likely contain information on their topic, give them a list of research questions and ask them to identify, from the library's list of periodical databases, which two databases will most likely contain articles on the topic. See example 5.1.

3. To clarify how field limiters can affect relevancy, have students compare and contrast the results of keyword searching in different fields. For example, compare the relevance of results when *binge drinking* is searched in the default field and the title field.

4. Illustrate the differences in results when searching by keyword and controlled vocabulary.

5. Ask students to read the descriptors of articles, and then have them identify those that closely approximate the relevancy of the article topic.

6. Compare the differences in results when searching a periodical database, Google, and a Web directory. Ask students to perform the same search in each, and then have them consider what aspects of the topic are covered, the types of sources included, and the ownership of sources.

7. Have students practice the comparative advantages and disadvantages of limiting a search to specific fields rather than searching full text.

8. Have students critique search strategies that have been done by other students.

9. One way to show students how scholars "talk" to one another is to have them trace the history of an article via citation indexes. This exercise will help them to understand the mechanics of citation searching as well as learn how others respond to the ideas of the original author. Students can examine how subsequent authors built upon the ideas or discoveries or replicated a study.

10. Students can research the scholarly contributions of a historian, literary critic, biologist, and so on—what they wrote and what others thought about it. They can write their findings and how they went about searching for the material.

INSTRUCTOR GUIDES, HANDOUTS, AND EXERCISES

1. Example 5.1: Choosing Relevant Databases, Exercise
2. Example 5.2: Search Strategy, Worksheet

Websites on Searching Periodical Databases

These online tutorials present various ways of guiding students through the basic steps of searching and locating articles in electronic databases. Tutorials that provide exercises are indicated. Most of these sites provide only basic Boolean or keyword search instruction. For sites that discuss complex Boolean search strategies, see chapter 3.

1. Cabrillo College Library, "Electronic Full-Text Databases: Special Search Features," www.topsy.org/Misc/ChaptersList.html. Provides a tutorial on search strategies with a follow-up exercise.

2. Chippewa Valley Technical College, "Searchpath: Finding Articles," www.cvtc.edu/Library/SearchPath/choice.html. An interactive practice session in *Academic Search Elite* accompanies an introduction to periodical databases.

3. Colorado Mountain College Library, "Using Subscription Online Databases to Find Articles," www.coloradomtn.edu/library/tutorials/ebsco/intro2.html. Graphic demonstration of basic search strategies. Also provides an exercise.

4. Duke University Libraries," Electronic Searching," www.lib.duke.edu/libguide/adv_searching.htm#Field. Detailed graphic guide to Boolean, field searching, proximity operators, and truncation.

5. Emmanuel College Library, "Tutorial: Finding Articles," www1.emmanuel.edu/library/pages/tutorials.html. PowerPoint presentation introducing students to periodical searching. Examples are drawn from *Academic Search Elite*. This site also delivers a tutorial on nursing research.

6. Five Colleges of Ohio, "Information Literacy Tutorial," www.denison.edu/collaborations/ohio5/infolit. Tutorial accompanied by exercises on the types and varieties of research databases and search strategies.

7. Fort Lewis College Library, "Introduction to Locating Research Materials in Periodicals," library.fortlewis.edu/instruct/lib150/default.asp?tcgCache=Go&. Provides tutorial and assignment requiring students to build a search strategy and perform the search.

8. Grinnell College Libraries, "Choosing Periodical Databases," www.lib.grinnell.edu/research/find/findarticles.html. Query-based guide to selecting appropriate periodical databases.

9. Heritage College Library, "Searching for Articles in Periodicals," www.cegep-heritage.qc.ca/menu-link/ilp.htm. An assignment (PDF) accompanies an *EbscoHost* tutorial.

10. Long Beach City College Library, "Tutorials," lib.lbcc.edu/tutorials.html. Graphic tutorial on searching online databases.

11. Louisiana State University Libraries, "Finding Periodical Articles," www.lib.lsu.edu/instruction/periodical/period00.html. Detailed tutorial on searching for periodical articles.

12. Maryville College, "Survival Skills for Library Research," faculty. maryvillecollege.edu/library/libexercises/frshorientation.htm. Provides an exercise designed to introduce freshmen to basic periodical research.

13. Moravian College Library, "Periodical Articles," home.moravian. edu/public/reevestutorial/pages/index.htm. Provides a tutorial on basic search strategies. Includes an exercise where students practice planning a search strategy.

14. Ohio State University Libraries, "Net Tutor," liblearn.osu.edu/tutor. Graphic tutorial includes quizzes.

15. Purdue University, "CORE: Comprehensive Online Research Education," gemini.lib.purdue.edu/core. Includes a pretest and quizzes.

16. Radford University, "Library Tutorial: Searching Electronic Databases," lib.radford.edu/Tutorial. Introduces users to the basics of searching periodical databases.

17. Janet Romine, "Lib. 111 Information Sources," www2.truman. edu/~jiromine/LIB111/lib111.html#Assignments. Includes assignments on periodical types and database searching.

18. Simon Fraser University, "Ecology Research Project: Library Tutorial," www.lib.sfu.ca/researchhelp/subjectguides/bisc/previous/ bisc102fall03.htm#articles. Focuses on the varieties of science periodicals and databases as well as basic search strategies.

19. University of Maryland. "Finding Articles: Using Library Databases," www.umuc.edu/library/database/articles.shtml. Basic tutorial focusing on database searching.

20. University of North Carolina Library, "Information Literacy Modules: Searching Databases and Evaluating Results," www.library. ncat.edu/ref/information_literacy/course/toc.htm. Tutorial includes examples drawn from *EbscoHost* and *Infotrac*. Includes quizzes.

21. University of Texas System Digital Library, "Tilt," tilt.lib.utsystem.edu. Innovative interactive tutorial on the library and Web resources. Includes exercises and quizzes.

22. University of Utah, Health Sciences Library, "Internet Navigator: Modules 3," www-navigator.utah.edu. This interactive tutorial provides two tracks. Track 1 focuses on general topics, and Track 2 is restricted to health-related topics. Provides assignments and quizzes.

23. University of Vermont Library, "Information and Instruction Services Quiz," bailey.uvm.edu/ref/hist12libexnew.html. Focuses on introductory-level history research in periodicals, books, and book reviews. An assignment is provided.
24. University of Victoria, "Library Tutorial: Find Journal Articles," gateway.uvic.ca/lib/instruction/ltut/default.html. Guides students through the search process using *Academic Search Elite.*
25. University of Washington. "Research 101," www.lib.washington.edu/uwill/research101/index.html. Tutorial on databases and database searching includes exercises and review quizzes.
26. University of Wisconsin, "Module 4: Finding Periodical Articles," perth.uwlax.edu/murphylibrary/tutorial/periodicals/start4.html. Provides a tutorial of the basics, including elementary keyword and Boolean searching. Includes an exercise.
27. University of Wyoming Libraries. "TIP: Tutorial for Information Power," tip.uwyo.edu/intro1.htm. Introductory tutorial accompanied by short quizzes.
28. Washington State University Libraries, "Finding Journals, Magazines, Newspapers," www.wsulibs.wsu.edu/electric/trainingmods/griffin_tutorial.

APPENDIX: EXAMPLES

Example 5.1: Choosing Relevant Databases, Exercise

For each of the following topics, choose the best and second best periodical database.

1. What is the correlation between academic achievement and children of divorce?
   Best choice _____
   Second best choice _____

2. Why do corporations offer physical fitness programs to their employees?
   Best choice _____
   Second best choice _____

3. Is TV violence to be blamed for the increased aggression in American culture?
Best choice _____
Second best choice _____

4. How did Mark Twain depict blacks in his novels?
Best choice _____
Second best choice _____

5. Review the issue of harvesting old-growth forests by the lumber industry.
Best choice _____
Second best choice _____

6. During World War II, did the United States have to bomb Hiroshima and Nagasaki?
Best choice _____
Second best choice _____

Example 5.2: Search Strategy, Worksheet

1. Develop a statement of your topic.
2. Divide the topic statement into concepts.
3. Select synonyms that express each concept.
4. Identify appropriate research databases.
5. Apply search strategy to the database.

NOTES

1. Craig Emerson and Michael Miyazaki, "Abstracting and Indexing Adapts to the Internet Era: A Publisher's Perspective," *Serials Review* 29 (2003): 222.

2. Carolyn G. Heilbrun, *Toward a Recognition of Androgyny* (New York: Knopf, 1973), 56.

3. Record excerpted from *EbscoHost's Academic Search Elite*.

6

ORGANIZATION OF KNOWLEDGE IN ACADEMIC LIBRARIES

Library books [were] promiscuous, ready to lie in the arms of anyone who asked.[1]

Goal: To recognize how recorded knowledge is organized in the library.
Objective 1: Explain the Library of Congress Classification (LCC) system.
Objective 2: Interpret a call number.

The card catalog might have gone gently into the night had it not been for novelist Nicholas Baker, who, in a 1994 *New Yorker* article, accused librarians of trashing the venerable card catalog, gleefully sacrificing scholarship and access for the glitz of the online public access catalog (OPAC).[2] Defending "the giant boxes and their scribbled-upon, dog-eared records,"[3] he later led a crusade to save the San Francisco Public Library's card catalog. While some librarians sided with Baker, most librarians agreed with Harvard librarian Malcolm Hamilton: "We threw our card catalogue away. It was a wrenching thing to do, but it was useless."[4]

Many seemed to assume that the online catalog, with its flexible multidimensional structure would improve users' ability to access books. However, as several studies on information-seeking behavior have shown, users still have problems getting what they want from an OPAC.[5] Some of these problems involve unfamiliarity with the content of online catalogs, ignorance of how OPACs process searches, failure to differentiate between keyword and subject searches, and ability to construct search strategies.

What Christine L. Borgman concluded in 1996 still holds true today: "Most end users of online catalogs are perpetual novices who lack the requisite conceptual knowledge for searching."[6] Compounding the problem, many online interfaces lull users into a false sense of security because they are deceptively simple. Some users believe that because they have found things in the past, they are successful at searching online catalogs and thus do not need formal instruction in how to use them.

LEARNING OBJECTIVES AND INSTRUCTOR ACTIVITIES

Objective 1: Explain the Library of Congress Classification (LCC) System.

Most students are hazy about the scheme by which university library books are arranged on the shelves. Beyond knowing that the peculiar system of letters and numbers on the spine of a book leads them to its place on the shelf, students give little thought to the organization of books in the library. And why should they? If they can pull the right book off the shelf, what else should they know? Yet, knowing the system libraries use helps students recognize the intellectual environment that surrounds the section in which the desired book is shelved. As William H. Wisner observes, "The arrangement of knowledge, . . . unaided and unlinked, is an impenetrable labyrinth."[7] Thus, students who are familiar with how academic libraries link recorded knowledge grasp how library collections reflect the "the construction of categories of knowing and the development of linkages between them."[8]

The scheme that most U.S. colleges and universities use to arrange their collections is the Library of Congress Classification (LCC) system, which was developed in the late nineteenth and early twentieth centuries. Conceptually based, LCC divides the intellectual contributions of humanity—ideas, concepts, creations, discoveries, and inventions—into twenty-one concept classes, using alphabetical letters to signify main classes such as philosophy, history, and science (see tables 6.1 through 6.3). This chapter's section on instructor guides, handouts, and exercises presents links to Library of Congress classification charts. Each of the LCC classes is broken down into specific subclasses. Within each class or subclass, class ranges further specify subject categories. LCC uses a combination of letters and numbers to designate these classes and subclasses.

LCC is very similar to supermarkets, recipe files, and the yellow pages. They each have a scheme to make meaning out of an otherwise chaotic jumble by grouping and classifying like things with other like things. Classification brings together similar items, whether books or groceries, so that users can access them easily on the shelves or in catalogs. Moreover, knowing the LCC system allows students to develop the habit

Table 6.1. Library of Congress Classification (LCC) System

A	General Works	M	Music
B	Philosophy/Psychology/Religion	N	Fine Arts
C	Auxiliary Science/History	P	Language/Literature
D	History/General/Europe	Q	Science
E	History/America	R	Medicine
F	History/America	S	Agriculture
G	Geography/Anthropology/Recreation	T	Technology
H	Social Sciences	U	Military Science
J	Political Science	V	Naval Science
K	Law	Z	Bibliography/Library Science

Table 6.2. Examples of LCC Subclasses

N	Fine Arts
NA	Architecture
NB	Sculpture
NC	Drawing/Design/Illustration

Table 6.3. Examples of LCC Class Ranges

E 441–453	Slavery in the United States/Antislavery movements
E 456–655	Civil War Period, 1861–1865
E 482–489	Confederate States of America

of browsing the books shelved in close proximity to a chosen book. Likewise, when the library's computer system crashes, knowing students will at least be aware of some class numbers related to their topic.

While browsing shelves is a powerful search method, it cannot supplant other search methods. For example, contrary to popular belief, all books on the same topic are not necessarily shelved in the same area. Students may not realize that a book's topic might crossover into other disciplines. Depending upon the emphasis, for example, books on alcoholism can be assigned to any number of subclasses: RC/RJ (medical), HD/HF (workforce), PN/PS (cinema, literature), and HV (social pathology). Likewise, no class has been defined to represent multiple topics covered in a monograph or a collection of essays, such as *Victorian Appropriations of Shakespeare, George Eliot, A. C. Swinburne, Robert Browning, and Charles Dickens*. Thus, to avoid overlooking key books, students should know to supplement browsing the shelves with searching the OPAC by subject (further explanation of this appears later this chapter).

Objective 2: Interpret a Call Number.

Call numbers reflect the dynamic system of LCC. The purpose of the call number is to help patrons find books quickly. The call number specifies the book's topic and location; each call number is unique to each book and is found on its spine and in its record in the online catalog.

Call numbers are important to patrons because they save time. Novice searchers often copy only the top two lines of a call number and then become frustrated when they realize they cannot find their book because one hundred other books have the same class number. Encourage students to copy the entire call number before they leave the terminal.

How Call Numbers Work   The best way to understand how to read a call number is to deconstruct one. Table 6.4 illustrates the parts of the call number for Debbie Nathan and Michael Snedeker's book *Satan's Silence: Ritual Abuse and the Making of a Modern American Witch Hunt*. Students often get LCC classes confused with LC subject headings (LCSH). It is probably best to not teach the concepts of each back to back in a library session. Table 6.5 describes the major differences between LCC and LCSH.

Table 6.4. Parts of a Call Number

HV	Social Pathology/Social and Public Welfare/Criminology
6626.52	Child Abuse
N379	Author number
1995	Publication year

Table 6.5. LCC vs. LCSH

LCC	LCSH
Locates books on shelves	Locates books on a topic
Expressed in letters and numbers	Expressed in words and phrases
Assigned one LC number	May have multiple headings

CLASS ACTIVITIES

One-Hour Sessions

1. Briefly compare the organizational schemes used in OPACs, Web directories (e.g., Google), and periodical databases.
2. For subject-specific sessions, point out or include in handouts or websites LCC classes and subclasses that relate to relevant subject areas. The following sections list websites that provide subject-specific LCC charts.

Multiple Sessions and Courses

1. To help students understand shelf order, write a set of call numbers on the board in random order. For example:

HV	HV	HV	HV	HV
22	25	25	25	22
V5413	F76	C8	R63	C6
1999	2003		1968	

Ask students to arrange them in proper call number order. See "Tools for Assessment" in this chapter for additional exercises and quizzes on call number order.
2. A great deal of time should not be spent on LCC and call numbers. Both concepts can be quickly demonstrated by diagramming a call number on the board. Briefly discuss each part, and reinforce

the idea that the call number is like a book's address: all parts are needed to retrieve the book.

3. For subject-specific sessions, point out the classes and subclasses that relate to relevant subject areas. The following sections list websites that provide subject-specific LCC charts.
4. Compare and contrast an LC call number with that of a DCC call number. This is especially useful for incoming freshmen.
5. Explore the different organizational schemes used in OPACs, Web directories (e.g., Google), and periodical databases.
6. To reinforce students' understanding of the LCC scheme, ask them to assign main classes and subclasses to a series of topics. See examples 6.1–6.4 for sample exercises.

INSTRUCTOR GUIDES, HANDOUTS, AND EXERCISES

1. Examples 6.1–6.2: LCC Main Classes, exercise and answer key
2. Examples 6.3–6.4: LCC Subclasses, exercise and answer key

Websites on LCC

These websites provide the LCC outline:

1. Florida Atlantic University Libraries, "Online Tutorial: Introduction to Call Numbers," www.library.fau.edu/depts/instsrv/tutorial/call5.htm#s. Provides thumbnail charts of each class and its subclasses.
2. Library of Congress, "Classification Outline," (July 5, 2005), www.loc.gov/catdir/cpso/lcco/lcco.html. Provides outline of main classes and subclasses.

These links provide charts comparing LCC, Dewey Decimal classification, and Superintendent of Documents (SuDoc):

1. Five Colleges of Ohio Library, "Information Literacy Tutorial: Understanding Call Numbers" (2000), www.denison.edu/collaborations/ohio5/infolit/c2libnav.

2. Louisiana State University Libraries, "Call Numbers and Interpretation" (August 23, 2006), www.lib.lsu.edu/instruction/callnumbers/callnum01.html.
3. University of Maryland University Library, "College Research Skills Tutorial: How Call Numbers Work" (2005), www.umuc.edu/library/tutor/mod4.html.

These websites provide explanations of interpreting LC call numbers and locating books on the shelf:

1. Cerro Coso College, "Understanding LC Call Numbers" (January 21, 2004), www.cerrocoso.edu/lrc/LC_Class/UnLC.htm. Detailed explanation of how to read a call number. Includes illustrations.
2. Honolulu Community College Library, "Understanding Call Numbers" (March 26, 2004), www.hcc.hawaii.edu/education/hcc/library/callno.html. Includes brief explanations with graphics.
3. Kansas State University Libraries, "Understanding LC Call Numbers" (May 2005), catnet.ksu.edu/help/lccn.html.
4. University of Michigan, "Searchpath: Call Numbers," www.lib.umich.edu/ugl/searchpath/glossary/index.html.
5. University of North Carolina, Wilmington Library, "Library Resource Guides" (September 6, 2006), library.uncw.edu/web/research/topic/callnumbers.html. Provides LCC chart, interpreting a call number and location of call numbers. Includes a list of reasons justifying shelf order.
6. Virginia Tech University Libraries, "Call Number Training" (2004), shelving.lib.vt.edu/call-number/index.html. Tutorial for training student assistants. Provides an easy-to-read chart explaining the position of call numbers on the shelves.

These websites chart LC classes by subject:

(Popular Topics) Boston Public Library, "Popular Subjects and Their Library of Congress Call Numbers" (2001), www.bpl.org/guides/popular.htm.
(American Studies) Skidmore College Library, "LC Call Numbers by Subject: American Studies" (2002), www.skidmore.edu/library/

subjects/lcc/lcc.htm. Includes call number ranges for several subject areas, including art, biology, history, and business.
(History) New York University Library, "LCC Tutorial for History," library.nyu.edu/research/history/tutorial/mod1d.htm. Provides a page of LC class numbers for history-related topics.
(Literature) Queens University Library. "World Literature Classes," 130.15.161.74/techserv/cat/Sect03/literaturelist.html.
(Music) University of California, Berkeley, Hargrove Music Library, "ML Literature on Music" (August 16, 2004), www.lib.berkeley.edu/MUSI/ml.html.
(Sciences) University of Notre Dame, University Libraries, "History and Philosophy of Science," www.library.nd.edu/colldev/policy/history_philosophy_science.shtml.
(Sciences) University of Oregon Libraries, "List of Science LC Classification Numbers" (August 15, 2006), libweb.uoregon.edu/scilib/handouts/class_s.html.
(Social Welfare) University of California, Berkeley, Social Welfare Library, "Significant Call Numbers in the Social Welfare Library" (April 20, 2004), www.lib.berkeley.edu/SOCW/socw_lccallnumbers.html.

Assessment Tools

1. LCC main classes and subclasses exercises and answer keys (examples 6.1–6.4)
2. Helena Dittman and Jane Hardy, Learn the Library of Congress Classification (Lanham, MD: Scarecrow, 2000). While primarily for library science students, many of the exercises can be adapted for other college students.

These websites provide quizzes on interpreting and locating call numbers.

1. American University Library, "Call Numbers Exercise," www.library.american.edu/tutorial/call_number3.html. Interactive exercise.
2. California State University, San Marcos Library, "Literature of Chemistry," library.csusm.edu/course_guides/chemistry/Chemistry.300.sp04.asp. Provides exercises in which students compare

the organizational schemes used in Google's directory and Scrius with MeSH and LCC.

3. Colorado State University Libraries, "Finding a Book on the Shelf" (August 21, 2006), lib.colostate.edu/howto/others/findb-klc.html. Includes quiz on correct order of call numbers.

4. East Carolina University, Joyner Libraries, "How Do I Read a Call Number?" www.ecu.edu/cs-lib/reference/display.cfm?id=26. Interactive quiz on call number order.

5. Indiana University, Bloomington, Libraries, "Shelving at the IUB Libraries: Library of Congress Classification System" (1998), www.indiana.edu/~libcirc/lcwww/lc.html.

6. Louisiana State University Library, "Call Numbers and Interpretation" (August 23, 2006), www.lib.lsu.edu/instruction/callnumbers/callnum01.html. Tutorial includes an exercise.

7. Sam Houston State University Library, "Understanding Call Numbers," library.shsu.edu/research/instruction/index.php. Multiple-choice quiz on LC classes, shelf order, cutter numbers, and so on.

8. University of Rhode Island Library, "Skills Tutorial: How to Read Shelf Numbers," www.uri.edu/library/tutorials/uri101/quiz/index.html. The quiz involves a series of out-of-place books in a graphic screen. The student is asked to drag drop them into their proper call number order.

9. University of Southern Indiana, David L. Rice Library, "Call Numbers" (2002), www.usi.edu/LIBRARY/howto.asp. Includes a call number quiz.

10. Western Connecticut State University Library, "Library of Congress Call Number Quiz" (May 31, 1997), people.wcsu.edu/reitzj/res/call-numbers.html. Includes an interactive quiz on LC call number order.

APPENDIX: EXAMPLES

Example 6.1: LCC Main Classes, Exercise

For each of the following topics, assign the appropriate LCC main class:

Topic	Main Class
court system	_____

geology   _____
Toni Morrison's novels   _____
origins of the Russian Revolution   _____
dinosaurs   _____
emergency care   _____
taxation   _____
Gospel music   _____
Fortune 500   _____
domestic violence   _____
high-speed rail   _____
Gettysburg Address (1863)   _____
Mayan culture   _____
melodrama   _____
Frida Kahlo   _____
Plato's ideas   _____
discipline in the classroom   _____
Muslim faith   .   _____
urban legends   _____
presidential campaigns   _____

Example 6.2: LCC Main Classes, Answer Key

For each of the following topics, assign the appropriate LCC main class:

Topic	Main Class
court system	K
geology	Q
Toni Morrison's novels	P
origins of the Russian Revolution	D
dinosaurs	Q
emergency care	R
taxation	H
Gospel music	M
Fortune 500	H
domestic violence	H
high-speed rail	T
Gettysburg Address (1863)	E

Mayan culture	F
melodrama	P
Frida Kahlo	N
Plato's ideas	B
discipline in the classroom	L
Muslim faith	B
urban legends	G
presidential campaigns	J

Example 6.3: LCC Subclasses, Exercise

Class H—Social Sciences   Each of the following topics belongs to the main class H. Using the list of H subclasses as a guide (www.loc.gov/catdir/cpso/lcco/lcco_h.pdf), assign each topic to its appropriate subclass.

Topic	Subclass
homeless shelters	_____
stock market crash of 1929	_____
biography of Karl Marx	_____
marketing to Gen Xers	_____
quantitative sociology	_____
gay culture	_____
alcohol and the community	_____
introduction to sociology	_____
single parenthood	_____
labor strikes	_____

Class P—Language and Literature   Each of the following topics belongs to the main class P. Using the list of P subclasses as a guide (www.loc.gov/catdir/cpso/lcco/lcco_p.pdf), assign each topic to its appropriate subclass.

Topic	Subclass
work of Mishima	_____
modernism in literature	_____
Pablo Neruda's poetry	_____
Spike Lee's films	_____
English grammar	_____

editions of the *Aeneid*   _____
dime novels of the American West   _____
sonnets of Shakespeare   _____
stage design and lighting   _____
Russian short stories   _____
Persian grammar   _____

Example 6.4: LCC Subclasses, Answer Key

Class H—Social Sciences   Each of the following topics belongs to the main class H. Using the list of H subclasses as a guide
(www.loc.gov/catdir/cpso/lcco/lcco_h.pdf), assign each topic to its
appropriate subclass.

Topic	Subclass
homeless shelters	HV
stock market crash of 1929	HB
biography of Karl Marx	HX
marketing to Gen Xers	HC
quantitative sociology	HM
gay culture	HQ
alcohol and the community	HV
introduction to sociology	HM
single parenthood	HQ
labor strikes	HD

Class P—Language and Literature   Each of the following topics belongs to the main class P. Using the list of P subclasses as a guide
(www.loc.gov/catdir/cpso/lcco/lcco_p.pdf), assign each topic to its appropriate subclass.

Topic	Subclass
work of Mishima	PL
modernism in literature	PN
Pablo Neruda's poetry	PQ
Spike Lee's films	PN
English grammar	PE
editions of the *Aeneid*	PA

dime novels of the American West	PS
sonnets of Shakespeare	PR
stage design and lighting	PN
Russian short stories	PG
Persian grammar	PK

NOTES

1. Elizabeth McCracken, *The Giant's House: A Romance* (New York: Dial, 1996), 252.

2. The old card catalog did not die; it just reinvented itself. People have appropriated them to hold odds and ends, store CDs, and serve as art. For instance, artist David Bunn has been creating installations from the two million catalog cards he rescued from the Los Angeles Public Library. Bunn's pieces "direct attention to their [cards'] strong poetic voice . . . [and embrace] their physicality, age, and obsolescence. He spins poems from the titles running across the tops of the cards, honors the catalog's systemic order and succinct formality, and credits the catalog with personality, history, ideology, and even an unconscious." (Leah Ollman, "Relics of the Material Age," *Art in America* [November 2000]: 134–39).

3. Nicholas Baker, "Card Catalogs Destroyed as Online Systems Grow," April 4, 1994, 64.

4. Andrea Neighbours, "From the Stacks to the Internet, Librarians Still Keep Up the Search," *Christian Science Monitor*, November 19, 1996.

5. These studies include Christine L. Borgman, "Why Are Online Catalogs Still Hard to Use?" *Journal of the American Society for Information Science* 47 (1996): 494; Tschera Harkness Connell, "Techniques to Improve Subject Retrieval in Online Catalogs: Flexible Access to Elements in the Bibliographic Record," *Information Technology and Libraries*, June 10, 1991, 87–98; Charles R. Hildreth, "The Use and Understanding of Keyword Searching in a University Online Catalog," *Information Technology and Libraries*, June 1997, 52–62; Monica Cahill McJunkin, "Precision and Recall in Title Keyword Searches," *Information Technology and Libraries*, September 1995, 161–65; and Fredrick Sclafani, "Controlled Subject Heading Searching versus Keyword Searching," *Technicalities* (October 1999): 7–15.

6. Borgman, "Why Are Online Catalogs Still Hard to Use?" 494.

7. William H. Wisner, "End of an Edifice," *Sewanee Review* 109 (2001): 226.

8. Wisner, "End of an Edifice," 226.

7

SEARCHING ONLINE PUBLIC ACCESS CATALOGS (OPACS)

Beware of the man of one book.[1]

> Goal: To search OPACs for relevant resources.
> Objective 1: Recognize the benefits of Library of Congress Subject Headings (LCSH) as a search tool.
> Objective 2: Use the red books (LCSH) to identify appropriate headings.
> Objective 3: Compare LCSH to keyword searching.
> Objective 4: Use LCSH and keyword strategies.
> Objective 5: Recognize when to search beyond OPACs.

Thomas Mann, in an *American Libraries* article, observes that librarians "need to get over the uncritical habit of regarding [Library of Congress subject headings] . . . as mere carryovers from the age of manual card catalogs." He argues that we need to consider LCSH "afresh in the light of their new and greatly increased powers to aid researchers in the online age."[2] Mann is quite correct in his observations that many librarians tend to minimize the effectiveness of Library of Congress (LC) subject headings when searching OPACs. It is hoped that this chapter will inspire librarians and other information specialists to reconsider the role of LCSH as an important search strategy.

LCSH emerged in the last decade of the nineteenth century to provide better access to its own collections. By the end of the twentieth century, LCSH had grown to approximately a quarter million terms and had become the most comprehensive nonspecialized controlled vocabulary in the English language.[3] Moreover, the LCSH system had been adopted by or used as a model for libraries worldwide, as well as provided subject access to online periodical databases, such as *Wilson-Web*, and Web directories, such as Infomine and Librarians Index, to the Internet.

The design of LCSH operates, not upon a theoretical construction of the universe of knowledge, but on an actual collection; that is, established headings are based on material received and cataloged by the Library of Congress. Like other controlled vocabularies, the conceptual framework of LCSH groups like books together (see table 7.1). LC catalogers attempt to assign headings—usually no more than six—that closely approximate the content of the book. Thus, the subject tracings provide a standardized description of the book's contents.

The LCSH vocabulary attempts to mirror the language change that accompanies cultural, social, and political shifts. Consider the changes in headings for Americans of African heritage: until the 1970s LC used

Table 7.1. Sample LCSH Entry

Business ethics (May Subd Geog) [HF5387]	
UF	Business people—Professional ethics
	Commercial ethics
	Corporate ethics
	Corporation ethics
BT	Professional ethics
RT	Wealth—Moral and ethical aspects
NT	Advertising in educational media
	Business intelligence
	Construction industry—Corrupt practices
	Corporations—Corrupt practices
	Courts of honor
	Executives—Conduct of life
	Nepotism
	Real estate development—Corrupt practices
	Social responsibility of business

Negroes; thereafter it was replaced with *Afro-Americans* and remained that way until 2000, when it was replaced with *African Americans*. Until the advent of online cataloging, LC was slow to change headings that were "variously antique, bizarre, clinical, embarrassing, and unhelpful."[4] Part of the reluctance to replace these headings was because, prior to automation, updating them was labor intensive and expensive. For example, according to Lynn M. El-Hosy, updating the archaic *moving-pictures* with *motion pictures* in 1987 involved revising catalog cards for approximately four hundred related headings and updating the subject headings assigned to thousands of card entries.[5] Hence, catalogers had to balance the benefits of replacing headings and the costs that it incurs. Today, decades do not have go by before outdated headings are replaced. Online cataloging has enabled LC to respond much quicker to changes in usage, as well as be more willing to establish terms for new topics.

In addition, LCSH has excluded, distorted, and marginalized certain topical areas that are biased toward a white, male, Western, Judeo-Christian model. As Hope A. Olson argues, because the LC subject headings reflect topics represented in material cataloged and received by LC, they "echo the mainstream and reject the margins. . . . What is left out of LCSH defines its boundaries and illustrates the culture it endorses and enforces."[6] For example, the topics "wicca" and "corporate welfare" are not recognized by LCSH, despite the fact that each has substantial extant literature. This contradicts the rules of assigning subject headings, which states "assign headings that are as specific as the topics they cover." Furthermore, LSCH can distort or shift meaning. For example, narrower terms for the subject heading "feminism" (NT) reflect a "peculiar picture of the concept." Excluded from the NT list are several aspects of feminism, such as radical, cultural, Marxist, and socialist perspectives. Also, terms representing race and ethnicity are absent, resulting in a list that's "dated, white, middle class, [and from the] liberal movement with a few in-your-face splinter groups. Moreover, none of the feminism works focusing on race or ethnicity are included."[7] LCSH has been a work in progress, "built by many hands," which may explain many of its inconsistencies, ambiguities, and subjectivities. Despite these weaknesses, it is an effective retrieval tool. Most librarians probably agree with Elaine Svenonius' summation of LCSH:

A grand old lady, she has been ever earnest in her aim to adapt to user's habitual ways of looking at things. . . . She has tried to remake herself in response to the criticism leveled at her [and] in her later years, she has become increasingly self-aware, apologetic about her inconsistencies and worried about keeping up. Her life, though not exemplary, has been one whose story is worth telling, both for its own sake and as it holds a mirror up to the history of subject language in the 20th century.[8]

For additional discussions on controlled vocabulary and keyword searching, see chapters 4 and 5.

LEARNING OBJECTIVES AND INSTRUCTOR ACTIVITIES

Objective 1: Recognize the Benefits of Library of Congress Subject Headings (LCSH) as a Search Tool.

There has been a great deal of discussion about the relevance of controlled vocabulary in online library catalogs. Many argue that standardized subject headings should be dropped because most users rely on keyword searching; thus controlled vocabulary fails to justify the expense of maintaining it. On the other hand, others argue that keyword searches often overlook relevant records, and a study supports this argument. Tina Gross and Arlene G. Taylor found that "if subject headings were to be removed from or no longer included in catalog records, users performing keyword searches would miss more than one third of the hits they currently retrieve."[9] Clearly, keyword searches are not always adequate in retrieving relevant records.

Users search OPACs for three reasons—to locate:

1. a known item, for example, a specific author, title, or series;
2. everything on a known item, for example, an author's or artist's oeuvre, various editions of a work, translations, and so on; and
3. a topic, for example, persons, places, and things.

In doing subject searches in OPACs, the user must recognize the power of the subject heading system in retrieving relevant material. For this reason, the objectives in this chapter focus on the strengths and weaknesses of LCSH and how it compares to keyword searching. Controlled vocabulary benefits students in three ways:

1. It brings together related books, eliminating the need to enter several keywords that express the same things. For example, using uncontrolled terms to retrieve books on senior citizens, a user would have to use several terms including, *elderly*, *aged*, and *retirees*.
2. It eliminates confusing and ambiguous terms. For example, a user enters *environment* as in "natural environment," but also retrieves the totally unrelated items "school environment" and "work environment." LCSH also distinguishes homographs (words that look the same but have different meanings). For example, LC headings clarify the term *seal*, which has multiple meanings:

   • seals (animals)
   • seals (numismatics)
   • seals (stoppers)
   • seals and labels (philately)

3. It promotes browsing. The LCSH links related headings by using "see also" references and "broader," "narrower," and "related" headings, thereby giving users some search options that they may have not foreseen.

Objective 2: Use the Red Books (LCSH) to Identify Appropriate Headings.

The strength of the red books is its ability to assist students "to discover the hidden relatedness" among phenomena.[10] Subject headings can augment a search as well as make it more precise. Title words are not always clear enough for a keyword search to be effective. The following are the three ways in which students can determine appropriate LC subject headings:

1. Students can identify subject headings from a known, relevant title, found either through its online record or via the CIP data (i.e., LC's Cataloging-in-Publication Data) located on the

copyright pages of books. Provided by LC for books not yet published, participating U.S. publishers include the CIP data to facilitate processing for libraries.

2. Students can browse the online LC subject displays for subheadings (e.g., "biography," "cross-cultural studies," and "sociological aspects"). Subheadings are used to specify a main heading and to represent its various aspects. Often, students will hit on a subdivision that they had not thought of before. For example, a student interested in Hitler's formative years might begin by scrolling through the array of subdivisions under the subject "Hitler." One obvious heading is "childhood and youth." But further browsing among the array of subdivisions yields other options such as "family."

3. Students can consult the red books or its online equivalent, Classification Web (classificationweb.net). The power of the red books is in the cross-references, which help students to be specific and precise in their searches. LCSH cross-references work three ways—through associative, hierarchical, and equivalence relationships:

- Associative relationships link terms via related terms (RT) and "see also" references;
- Hierarchical relationships link terms conceptually by classing them as broader (BT) or narrower (NT). A common assumption among students using controlled vocabularies is that a BT will retrieve NTs. Remind students that a BT will not retrieve books dealing with topics listed under NT terms. Each term has to be entered individually.
- Equivalence relationships link unauthorized headings (Use or UF) to authorized subject terms.

Additionally, looking at adjacent entries may help to identify appropriate headings.

The red books' NTs counter a student's tendency to search too broadly. As many a reference librarian can attest, students often sacrifice an NT for a BT, for example, entering *television* when what they really want are books on reality television. The general heading entries can provide direction for students. For instance, a student starts out interested in business ethics but after perusing the hierarchical terms, he or she decides to focus on nepotism. Thus, the associative and hierarchical relationships can guide students to topics that they may not have foreseen or been aware of.

Objective 3: Compare LCSH to Keyword Searching.

While many LCSH searches result in high precision and recall, there are instances where users fare better executing keyword searches. The following highlights some of the situations where LCSH can hinder a search.

No Headings Are Equivalent to Title Words or Words Chosen by Users. How does this happen? First, LC often responds slowly to new phenomena. Catalogers rarely establish new headings until they are satisfied that there is enough material to warrant a new heading. Until a topic gets its own heading, catalogers will assign broader headings. For example, gangsta music lacks its own heading; books on this topic are usually assigned the broader heading "rap (music)."

Subject Headings Do Not Conform to Words and Phrases Users Will Likely Use. For example, the concept "people skills" is used frequently in public discourse. Consider the following titles and requisite LC headings:

* *The Complete Guide to People Skills* by Sue Bishop
  communication in personnel management
  communication in management
  interpersonal communication
  interpersonal relations

* *Cultural Intelligence: People Skills for Global Business*
  business anthropology
  management—cross-cultural studies
  corporate culture
  intercultural communication

* *Managing Diversity: People Skills for a Multicultural Workplace*
  diversity in the workplace

- *Teacher as Decision Maker: Real-Life Cases to Hone Your People Skills*
  teachers—United States—case studies
  teaching—case studies
  education—United States—decision making—case studies
  interaction analysis in education—case studies
  interpersonal relations—case studies

Note the absence of "people skills" as an LC heading; yet all four books have the phrase embedded in their titles. Moreover, observe the subject headings for each title: none have headings in common with one another, although two share "interpersonal relations." Hence, the only way that these titles can be retrieved as a set is by executing a phrase search in the title field. Clearly this is a case where keyword searching trumps controlled vocabulary because the words in titles often agree with terms searchers select. However, even this keyword search on people skills can bring lots of irrelevant hits if the user does not know to search it as a bound phrase. If entered as an unbound phrase, most interfaces will interpret it as: people AND skills; subsequently, the search set looks much different, and books like the following examples will be retrieved:

The Penobscot Dance of Resistance: Tradition in the History of a People
Essential Knowledge and Skills for Baccalaureate Social Work Students in Gerontology

Clearly these titles have nothing do with the art of interacting with people. Further, keyword searches often overwhelm the searcher with too many irrelevant hits because the system does not distinguish the different senses a word can have. For example, a student enters the term *seniors*, as in elderly, and the resulting search set is muddled with titles dealing with high school seniors.

Users Search the OPAC as If It Were a Periodical Database.   Users search too specifically by combining too many words, for example:

development of nursing schools in America
Queen Elizabeth and her ladies in waiting

These search strings are too complex too appear in titles of books or in LC subject headings. In addition, complex keyword strategies especially do not work in small OPACs and those that lack searchable contents fields (i.e., 505). These kinds of searches indicate users are unskilled at constructing logical searches. Complex search strings often reflect the exact phrasing used by their instructors in lectures, syllabi, and assignments. Or, the long strings of words are pulled from students' research questions or thesis statements. Underlying these kinds of searches is the common belief among students that if their exact topic or thesis is not expressed in the title of the book, it is useless. Such narrow thinking deprives the student of accessing potentially useful information. Yet, as experienced researchers know, useful discussions on one's topic can be buried within a book that discusses a broader context of an issue, a historical event, or the lives of other people. Thus, students should be encouraged when searching the OPAC to imagine that the book possibly could contain useful information.

LCSH's peculiarities in grammar and syntax may confuse users. For example, the headings "religion and sociology" and "hospitals—sociological aspects" deal with the sociological perspective of their respective nouns. It would be more consistent if headings such as these were constructed so that the noun was qualified by the same subdivision, either "sociology" or "sociological aspects."[12]

Objective 4. Use LCSH and Keyword Strategies.

Like periodical-database searching, no one search strategy fits all research queries. Effective searching of online library catalogs uses a combination of search strategies such as:

- beginning with a keyword/phrase search, determining relevant LC subject headings, and then using those to locate additional relevant titles. For example, *battered women* retrieves a few titles, yet many will be overlooked because LC catalogs them under "wife abuse," "abused wives," and "abused women";
- building a Boolean search using a combination of keywords and LC subject forms;
- searching the OPAC's browse displays of LCSH. Browse displays provide users with research options that they would not

have found via keyword or Boolean searches. In addition, unlike the LCSH red books, browse displays bring together free-floating subdivisions for a specific subject heading. For example: "motion pictures for women" is the formal LCSH heading, yet when translated into Boolean, it would read thus: motion pictures AND women;

- consulting the LCSH (red books) or its online version, Classification Web (classificationweb.net).

Objective 5: Recognize When to Search beyond OPACs.

Where does one go if one is looking for the published works of the Raelians, a fringe group who claimed they cloned a human being. Their work is likely not to be in library catalogs, as the publisher is nonmainstream and therefore not found in blurbs or other traditional collection development tools. By accessing Amazon.com, a simple keyword search indicates that *The True Face of God* was authored by Rael and published by the Raelian Foundation in 2003. Not only does Amazon sell copies, but one can also get a look at the first few pages of the book through their "Search inside the Book" program. While the online bookstore provides records for mainstream presses, researchers can also find books published by small presses, vanity presses, and so on.

CLASS ACTIVITIES

Design assignments and class activities that stress subject searching, especially in the use of LCSH. For sample LC heading questions, see example 7.3; for sample subject searches, see example 7.5.

One-Hour Sessions

Because there is little time to discuss any search method in detail, demonstrating via real life scenarios can show students how to approach subject searching conceptually. These scenarios show searching in action and reinforce the "hidden relatedness" of subject phenomena.

Scenario No. 1: Search Based on a Known Book

INSTRUCTOR: Pretend you are researching a paper about cults and ritual abuse. Your professor recommends you start with Nathan and Snedeker's book *Satan's Silence: Ritual Abuse and the Making of the Modern American Witch Hunt*. So where do you go to find the book?

CLASS: [response varies depending upon students' level of expertise].

INSTRUCTOR: Okay, so we will search the library's online catalog to determine whether we have the book. What is the quickest search method of finding this book?

CLASS: Title? Author?

INSTRUCTOR: Entering the title is the quickest route; however, you could still find it by entering the authors' names [retrieve the record and examine pertinent fields with class]. Now, this book looks good but you need more like it. How do you find them?

CLASS: [various responses].

INSTRUCTOR: The answer is in the record. First, notice that Nathan's book has bibliographical references. Make sure to peruse these for additional material. Second, to find relevant books follow the trail of the subject headings—they will often lead you to additional books [explain and demonstrate by following subject heading links].

Scenario No. 2: Search Based on a Combination of Keywords and LCSH

INSTRUCTOR: What happens if you are starting your research cold, with no recommendations? Let's pretend you are researching the topic, "relationship of the Catholic Church and Hitler's regime." If we enter this topic the way we have stated it, we will retrieve zero hits [if there is time, demonstrate]. Why? Because no book record contains all of the words in the search query. Therefore, we need to frame a search query that the OPAC will understand [write the topic statement on the board]. Now what is one important concept?

CLASS: Catholic Church.

INSTRUCTOR: Good, but do you want all books on the Catholic Church?

CLASS: No.

INSTRUCTOR: You want only those books that deal with . . .

CLASS: Hitler's regime

INSTRUCTOR: Okay. So let's try entering the query, "Hitler's regime catholic church." Uh oh, still no hits. What to do? Well, you do not go to the instructor and tell her there are no books on this topic. Instead you ask, "Why did this search query fail?"

CLASS: [often blank looks].

INSTRUCTOR: It's the fluff words that are throwing the search. For example, by using *Hitler's regime*, we assume it will be embedded in all relevant records dealing with the Catholic Church. But, what happens if other phrases are used instead, such as *Hitler's dictatorship*, *Hitler's government, Hitler's administration*, and so on? Thus, *regime* nor any other qualifier is needed because they are implied when Hitler is connected to the concept "Catholic Church." Furthermore, *church* is a fluff word also. Again, relevant material is missed because book titles and subject headings may use only *Catholic* or *Catholicism*. So, all we really need is *Catholic* and *Hitler* [enter search with appropriate truncation]. As a result, the OPAC retrieves two books: John Cromwell's *Hitler's Pope: The Secret History of Pius XII* and Lawrence D. Walker's *Hitler Youth and Catholic Youth, 1933–1936: A Study in Totalitarian Conquest*. They both look promising. But your research does not end here because several relevant books would be overlooked. To pursue these books, you will follow the trail of LCSH. For example, click on the relevant subject headings assigned to Cromwell's book, such as "Pius Pope, 1876–1956." As you can see, relevant LCSHs lead you to additional sources. [Note: If there is time, you can then demonstrate how to retrieve more books by using Boolean strategies. For example, (Hitler OR Nazi OR Reich) AND (Catholic OR pope OR papacy).]

Follow up these strategies with having students develop search queries based on their own topics. As a guide, provide a worksheet (see example 7.1).

MULTIPLE SESSIONS AND COURSES

1. To help students gain experience, provide several real-life scenarios, based on those under "One-Hour Sessions." Present students with a topic, and have them work out search strategies using a combination of keyword, controlled vocabulary, and Boolean.

2. Generally, students fail to grasp the advantages of using the red books unless they have hands-on experience. However, this proves

difficult, for most libraries have a limited number of LCSH sets. To help students visualize how LCSH can help them, replicate a page that pertains to their subject area. Then demonstrate the process of entering an LCSH term in the OPAC.

3. Include LSCH headings pertinent to a specific subject area in pathfinders, handouts, and websites. For an example, go to Indiana State University, "LCSH for Medical Economics/Ethics and Related Issues."

INSTRUCTOR GUIDES, HANDOUTS, AND EXERCISES

1. Examples 7.1–7.2: LCSH vs. Keywords, exercise and answer key
2. Examples 7.3–7.4: LC Subject Headings, exercise and answer key
3. Example 7.5: Sample OPAC Subject Searches

Websites on LCSH

The following sources provide basic instruction in LCSH:

1. Julie Banks and Susan Higgerson, "Conceptual and Mechanical Aspects of Subject Headings: A Brochure," *Show-Me Libraries* (Winter 1990): 25–29. In response to students' difficulty in using LC headings, the authors developed a brochure to increase subject search success rate. Includes a reprint of the brochure.
2. Colorado State University Library, "Library of Congress (LC) Subject Headings," lib.colostate.edu/howto/lcsh.html. Explanation of LCSH includes examples and brief exercise.
3. Duke University Libraries, "Library of Congress Subject Headings," www.lib.duke.edu/libguide/fi_books_sh.htm. Brief graphic explanation of LCSH.
4. Library of Congress, "Basic and Boolean Searching," (September 3, 2003), catalog.loc.gov/help/combinedsearch.htm. Provides a tutorial on searching LC's online catalog.
5. Library of Congress, "Classification Web," classificationweb.net. The online equivalent to the LCSH. Tutorial is included.

6. Northern State University, Williams Library, "Information Literacy Tutorial: Lesson Two" (2004), lib.northern.edu/infolit/tablesversion/home.htm. Tutorial includes quiz.

7. Purdue University Libraries, "Module 5: Subject Searching (Controlled Vocabulary)," www.lib.purdue.edu/vetmed/inst/supersearcher/module5.html. Provides comparisons of LCSHs with controlled vocabulary in other types of databases.

8. State University of New York, Binghamton Libraries, "What Are LC Subject Headings?" (June 2004), library.lib.binghamton.edu/guides/PDF/lcsh.pdf. Provides clear explanations, with many examples, of the purpose and use of LCSH. Includes a list of the most commonly used subheadings.

9. University of Mississippi Library, "Online Catalog Tutorial," www.olemiss.edu/depts/general_library/files/bi/leveltwo/booksmedia.htm. Includes title, author, keyword, subject searching, and the use of limiters. Graphic displays accompany explanations.

10. University of Oregon Library, "Library of Congress Subject Headings," libweb.uoregon.edu/guides/findbooks/subjects.html. Includes a list of the most commonly used subheadings.

11. University of Wisconsin, Milwaukee, Library, "Using Subject Headings," www.uwm.edu/Libraries/guides/subhd49.htm. Provides explanations of headings and types of subheadings, accompanied with examples.

The following sources explore OPAC search strategies.

1. K. Brodsky, "Library and Information Research: Humanities: Assignment 2," libweb.sonoma.edu/brodsky/292/assign2.html. Exercise on interpreting entries in LCSH.

2. California State University, Chico, "Keyword vs. Subject Searching in the Library Catalog," www.csuchico.edu/lins/assignments/keyword.doc. Exercise on linking free text terms to LCSH.

3. College of San Mateo Library, "Subject Searching" (2005), www.smccd.net/accounts/webready/lesson10_subject.asp. Provides exercises in basic search strategies, including searching LCSH.

4. Jacki Ganendran, *Learn Library of Congress Subject Access* (Lanham, MD: Scarecrow, 2000). Although primarily for students of

cataloging, this source provides several exercises as well as answer keys that could be adapted for non–library science students. Several of the exercises focus on determining acceptable LCSHs.

5. Heritage College Library, "Student Guide to Searching In-House Library Materials" (2006), www.cegep-heritage.qc.ca/Institution/Services/LibraryServices. Includes a detailed graphic tutorial on OPAC search strategies and a follow-up assignment.

6. Mount Mercy College Library, "LCSH and Finding Books: A Worksheet" (2000), www.mtmercy.edu/lib/blwksh2.htm. Provides an exercise in which students research LCSHs related to their topics.

7. Richland Community College, Kitty Lindsay Learning Resources Center, "Exercise for English 102," www.richland.edu/lrc/lrcexercise2005.pdf. Includes exercise on keyword and LCSH searching.

8. University of Adelaide Library, "Searching for Books on a Topic," www.adelaide.edu.au/library/guide/sci/Generalsci/tutref/section4.html. Tutorial includes an exercise.

9. University of Mississippi, "Online Catalog Tutorial," www.olemiss.edu/depts/general_library/files/bi/catindex.html. Includes title, author, keyword, subject, and the use of limiters. Graphic displays accompany explanations.

10. University of Wisconsin, Green Bay Library, "SearchPath," www.uwgb.edu/library/SearchPath/choice.html. Graphic tutorial on searching the library's OPAC.

11. Weber State University, Stewart Library, "Subject Searching," library.weber.edu/il/courses/ls2201/ac/assignment2.cfm. Includes an assignment on LCSHs and keyword searching.

APPENDIX: EXAMPLES

Example 7.1: LCSH vs. Keywords, Exercise

One advantage of using such controlled vocabulary as LCSH is that it brings together records on topics that can be expressed in diverse ways. For each of the following keywords, determine the corresponding LCSH(s).

1. Keywords: soda, sodas, soda pop, Coke, soft drinks
2. Keyword phrases: World War 1, World War I, World War One, Great War
3. Keywords: dot-coms, Web stores, online businesses
4. Keyword phrases: voting rights of women, women's right to vote
5. Keyword: electric cars
6. Keyword phrase: "Big Brother" (i.e., government's control of its citizens' private lives)
7. Keyword phrases: nuclear waste dumps, nuclear waste disposal, nuclear waste sites
8. Keyword phrases: binge eating, food addicts, food obsession, craving
9. Keyword phrases: movie reviews, film reviews

Example 7.2: LCSH vs. Keywords, Answer Key

One advantage of using such controlled vocabulary as LCSH is that it brings together records on topics that can be expressed in diverse ways. For each of the following keywords, determine the corresponding LCSH(s).

1. Keywords: soda, sodas, soda pop, Coke, soft drinks
   [suggested LCSH: carbonated beverages]
2. Keyword phrases: World War 1, World War I, World War One, Great War
   [suggested LSCH: World War, 1914–1918]
3. Keyword: dot-coms, Web stores, online businesses
   [suggested LCSH: electronic commerce///Internet industry]
4. Keyword phrase: voting rights of women, women's right to vote
   [suggested LCSH: women-suffrage///U.S. Constitution. 19th Amendment]
5. Keyword: electric cars
   [suggested LCSH: automobiles, electric]
6. Keyword phrase: "Big Brother" (i.e., government's control of its citizens' private lives)
   [suggested LCSH: privacy, right of///computer security///electronic surveillance]

7. Keyword phrases: nuclear waste dumps, nuclear waste disposal, nuclear waste sites
   [suggested LCSH: radioactive waste disposal///radioactive waste repositories]
8. Keyword phrases: binge eating, food addicts, food obsession, craving for food
   [suggested LCSH: compulsive eating///bulimia]
9. Keyword phrases: movie reviews, film reviews
   [suggested LCSH: Motion Picture—Reviews]

Example 7.3: LC Subject Headings, Exercise

1. What is the proper LC subject heading for the Day of the Dead?
2. The library has hundreds of books about Chicanos. What is the proper LC subject heading for this topic?
3. There are lots of books that deal with the origins of World War II. Identify one LC heading assigned to this topic?
4. Name at least two LC subject headings for books on battered women.
5. Many books that deal with the moral issues of the death penalty will be assigned the LC subject heading:_____
6. Find a book that discusses the theme of insanity in literary works. What relevant LC subject headings have been assigned to these books?
7. Locate a literary history for the English novel. What are the LC subject headings assigned to this book?
8. All the books listed under the LC heading "gun control" have been checked out. However, you can find books under closely related LC subject headings. Identify one LC subject heading.
9. Pretend that all the critical monographs on the following authors have been checked out. List related subject headings that might list books that have chapters or sections discussing the authors' works. Do not list LC headings that include the authors' names.

Jack Kerouac's work
Samuel Richardson's eighteenth-century novel *Clarissa*
Toni Morrison's novels

Example 7.4: LC Subject Headings, Answer Key

1. All Souls' Day
2. Mexican Americans
3. World War, 1939–1945—causes
4. abused women///wife abuse
5. capital punishment—moral and ethical aspects
6. Stephen Harper, *Insanity, Individuals, and Society in Late Medieval English Literature: The Subject of Madness* (New York: Edwin Mellen, 2003).
   literature and mental illness—England—history—to 1500
   mental illness in literature
   mentally ill in literature
7. John Richetti, *The Columbia History of the British Novel* (New York: Columbia University, 1994).
   English fiction—history and criticism
8. firearms—laws and legislation
9. Jack Kerouac's work
   Beat generation

   Samuel Richardson's eighteenth-century novel *Clarissa*

   epistolary fiction, English—history and criticism
   letter writing in literature
   letters in literature

   Toni Morrison's novels

   African American women in literature
   mother and child in literature
   mothers in literature
   motherhood in literature
   race relations in literature</ext>

Example 7.5: Sample OPAC Subject Searches

These searches help students build Boolean search strategies using keywords and LC subject headings. Note: "*" is the symbol for truncation.

1. Do a simple search for books dealing with Hitler. How many items are listed?
2. Narrow your search by locating books that deal with Hitler and the Catholic Church. Perform the search using Boolean.
   Suggested search strategy: (Hitler° OR Nazi° OR reich) AND (Catholic° OR pope° OR Pius OR Vatican)
3. Do a simple search for books discussing the work of Shakespeare. How many items are listed?
4. Narrow your search by locating books that deal with Shakespeare but limited to the concept of "women." Perform the search using Boolean.
   Suggested search strategy: Shakespeare° AND (women° OR female° OR femin°)

NOTES

1. Wolfgang Mieder, ed. *A Dictionary of American Proverbs* (New York: Oxford University Press, 1992), s.v. "Book."

2. Thomas Mann, "Why LC Subject Headings Are More Important Than Ever," *American Libraries* (October 2003): 52. The debate over LCSH continues. A 2006 report released by the Library of Congress suggests that LC eliminate LCSH. In his critical review of the report, Thomas Mann asserts that "Scholars throughout the country continue to regard browsing library book collections arranged in subject classified order as essential to their research; this fact is confirmed repeatedly in a variety of user studies." For the full-text reports, see Karen Calhoun, *The Changing Nature of the Catalog and Its Integration with Other Discovery Tools: Final Report, Library of Congress*, March 17, 2006, www.loc.gov/catdir/calhoun-report-final.pdf; and Thomas Mann, *What Is Going On at the Library of Congress?*, Library of Congress Professional Guild (AFSCME 2910), June 19, 2006, www.guild2910.org/AFSCME-WhatIsGoingOn.pdf.

3. Lois Mai Chan and Theodora Hodges, "Entering the Millennium: A New Century for LCSH," *Cataloging and Classification Quarterly* 29, nos.1 and 2 (2000): 226.

4. Sanford Berman, "Not Funny Anymore," *Library Journal*, June 1, 1988, 80.

5. Lynn M. El-Hoshy, "Charting a Changi ng Language with LCSH," *LC Information Bulletin* (August 1998), www.loc.gov/loc/lcib/9808/lcsh-lan.html.

6. Hope A. Olson, "Difference, Culture and Change: The Untapped Potential of LCSH," *Cataloging and Classification Quarterly* 29, nos. 1 and 2 (2000): 56, 59.

7. Olson, "Difference, Culture and Change," 57, 59.

8. Elaine Svenonius, "LCSH: Semantics, Syntax and Specificity," in *The LCSH Century: One Hundred Years with the Library of Congress Subject Headings System*, ed. Alva Stone (Haworth, 2000), 18.

9. Tina Gross and Arlene G. Taylor, "What Do We Have to Lose? The Effects of Controlled Vocabulary on Keyword Searching Results," *College and Research Libraries* 66, no. 3 (May 2005): 223. See also an earlier related study by H. J. Voorbij, "Title Keywords and Subject Descriptors: A Comparison of Subject Search Entries of Books in the Humanities and Social Sciences," *Journal of Documentation* 54, no. 4 (September 1998): 466–76.

10. William H. Wisner, "End of an Edifice," *Sewanee Review* (Spring 2001), voyager.lib.csub.edu:2092/resultlist.asp.

11. Library of Congress' Classification Web (classificationweb.net) is a web-based cataloging and referencing tool that enables users to access LC subject headings thesaurus style.

12. Jan Wepsiec, "Language of the Library of Congress Subject Headings Pertaining to Society," *Library Resources and Technical Services* 25 (April 1981): 199.

RESEARCHING BOOK REVIEWS

An enlightening book review is both science and art.[1]
There are books of which the backs and covers are by far the best
portion.[2]

Goal: To know how to evaluate a book.
Objective 1. Evaluate a book by its internal features.
Objective 2. Evaluate a book by its content.
Objective 3. Locate scholarly evaluations of books.

In cyberspace, everyone can become a critic; as one author comments, "It used to be that everyone had a book in them; today everyone has a book critic in them."[3] Nowhere is this more apparent than Amazon.com's controversial "customer reviews." At its best, it provides a forum for which readers can bypass established critical forms and anonymously voice alternative perspectives. At its worst, readers trash or rave about books based on incompetent reasoning and bias. The ugly side of anonymous reviewing was revealed in February 2004 when Amazon.com inadvertently posted the identities of anonymous commentators. Apparently, authors, in attempt to boost sales, had friends write—or they themselves had written—

anonymous reviews touting their own books. For example, novelist John Rechy gave himself a glowing review, signing himself as "a reader from Chicago." When he was outed, he reportedly laughed, saying, "That anybody is allowed to come in and anonymously trash a book to me is absurd. . . . How to strike back? Just go in and rebut every single [reviewer]."[4] In an attempt to protect against reviewer fraud and the quality of its product, Amazon no longer accepts anonymous reviews; reviewers must establish their identity with a credit card. But beyond biased reviewing, the sales, or the bottom line, engender the importance of consumer opinion of books.

To determine the best product, whether it be a watermelon or a healthcare plan, we as consumers rely on a variety of sources: friends, family, chat room buddies, product-rating sources, and advertisements. Consumers consult these sources with the hope of getting the edge on the best product. Likewise, skeptical researchers use a variety of sources to appraise the scholarly value of a book: they may consult colleagues, elicit comments from professional listservs, and seek out book reviews. The latter especially is an important component to the scholarly communication process. Upon a book's publication, scholars and professors react to it in several ways. They may comment on it initially through book reviews and review essays and later incorporate data from the book into an article or monograph they are writing or into the lectures they deliver. Moreover, book reviews promote scholarship and help professors and scholars keep abreast of what is new in their field.

Students use book reviews much differently than their instructors. Many students have little experience with reviews beyond those in *People* magazine or the "customer reviews" that Amazon.com posts. The latter especially reinforces the belief that all opinions are privileged, but as students become acquainted with well-written, thoughtful book reviews, they begin to realize that that not all opinions are privileged and that, while everyone is entitled to his or her opinion, these opinions are useless unless backed by careful judgment.

LEARNING OBJECTIVES AND INSTRUCTOR ACTIVITIES

The art of determining the authority and usefulness of a book involves two processes: scrutinizing the book's internal features (objective 1) and assessing the value of its content (objective 2).

Objective 1: Evaluate a Book by Its Internal Features.

While a book's internal features do not reveal the authoritativeness of a book, they help to ascertain whether the book is scholarly. Unlike popular books, most scholarly books contain a preface, foreword, introduction, or any combination of these three; copious notes; works cited; and possibly a bibliography, review of the literature, or bibliographical essay. Tables 8.1 and 8.2 delineate the title page and other front matter of a book. Each piece of the front matter reveals a part of the "character" of a book. Asking questions about these pieces can reveal a great deal about the internal features of a book.

Who Is the Author?
- What are his or her credentials?
- Is he or she trained in the area covered by the book?
- Has he or she published other materials?

Table 8.1. What the Title Page Reveals

Information on Title Page	What the Information Says about a Book
Title, subtitle, author	Describes book's content and identifies author
Publisher	Different types of publishers (e.g., university, commercial, trade, society, subsidized, vanity)
Edition	Various types of editions (e.g., monograph, anthology, festschrift, revised, reprint)
Date	May indicate both publication date and copyright dates

Table 8.2. Additional Front Matter

Front Matter	Purpose	Usefulness
Acknowledgments	Lists individuals and institutions that assisted the author	Identifies experts, archives, and collections the author consulted
Preface/Foreword	Explains purpose, origins of book, intended audience, coverage, what is excluded, and biases of the author	determines if book is relevant to the needs of the researcher
Table of Contents	Indicates organization of information	Identifies key points of the book
Introduction	Introduces thesis and discusses the treatment or approach	Provides overview of the book's content

Answers to these questions may be found in basic reference tools such as:

- Marquis Who's Who series
- *Contemporary Authors*
- *Directory of American Scholars*

In addition, students may explore whether the author's work has been discussed by others. An excellent place to start searching is by entering the author's name as subject in relevant periodical databases. If authors' profiles mention professional memberships, the following sources can help determine author's interests and perspectives:

- *Encyclopedia of Associations* (Thomson Gale)
- Associations on the Net (www.ipl.org/div/aon)
- Scholarly Societies Project (www.scholarly-societies.org)

What Does the Publication Date and Edition Tell Me? How old is the book? For some disciplines, reading dated material can be hazardous. This is especially true in the sciences, where advances in research nullify older information. However, older research in the humanities often is as relevant now as it was when it was first published. Nonetheless, students should be reminded that any material gleaned from older books should be verified with more current research. Another clue to the currency of a book is its edition. If a book has been revised and published again, subsequent substantial revisions indicate that information has been updated, mistakes have been rectified, and new material has been incorporated. Books that have undergone several editions may indicate a standard in the field.

What Does the Publisher Tell Me? Most students are not aware of the different types of publishers, ranging from university to academic to commercial to vanity. While most books published by university presses can be considered scholarly, one cannot automatically assume that they are free of errors or poor research and methodology. For more on verifying and corroborating sources, see chapter 10. Following are basic resources that provide information about publishers:

- *International Directory of Small Presses and Little Magazines* (W. W. Norton)
- *Publisher's Directory* (Thomson Gale)
- *Research Centers and Services Directory* (DialogWeb)
- *Research Centers Directory* (Thomson Gale)
- *International Research Centers Directory* (Thomson Gale)
- *Literary Market Place (LMP)* (Information Today)
- *The Writer's Market* (Writer's Digest Books)

Table 8.3 describe a book's back matter and how the information found here can prove useful to the student.

Objective 2: Evaluate a Book by Its Content.

Novice researchers rarely question the authority of a book. They assume that the author's arguments are well reasoned and supported by an ample amount of evidence. But as seasoned researchers know, this is a false assumption, even with scholarly sources. Some books are replete with factual errors, illogical arguments, or arguments unsupported by adequate data. Using this material can adversely affect the quality of students' papers, not to mention their standing with their instructors. So, how do undergraduates ascertain the authority of book? Without advanced degrees, how can they avoid using sources that may embarrass them academically? One obvious answer is to encourage them to read critiques of books by experts in the field. Book reviews can assist students in determining how:

- documentation is handled (or mishandled);
- the book fits within a canon or field of inquiry;
- a book contributes to scholarship;
- content fits into prevailing theories, ideas, and trends;
- arguments may be used to support or refute an assertion;

Table 8.3. Back Matter of a Book

Back Matter	Purpose	Usefulness
Endnotes, Footnotes, References	Explains text and cites sources	Follows up on data used to substantiate assertions or facts; lists sources for research project

- key scholars, experts, and research in the field affects a book; and
- controversies, debates, and disagreements pertain to a book.

While a book review can be a powerful tool in determining the credibility of a source, it is important to impress upon students that they should examine multiple reviews. As with film reviewers, academic reviewers disagree with each other and approach content with different perspectives. Examining two or more reviews will most likely protect the student from biased or poorly written critiques. Unfortunately, the scholarly community is not immune to bad reviewers. Some reviewers have specific agendas embedded in their reviews; others want to show off their intellectual superiority or ingratiate themselves with the author; and still others seek revenge to compensate for slights or to suppress competition. Some, as Chekhov observes, just want "buzz," as if to say, "See, I can buzz too, buzz about anything."[5] Yet, as David Henige points out in his provocative article on the "psycho-politics" of book reviewing, most scholarly reviews avoid these extremes and attempt to structure the review: "A few sentences set the stage, followed by a brief description, and perhaps, an analysis of the book's contents and arguments. Then, for balance, a few nits are picked, to be succeeded by a 'despite these, this is a useful contribution to knowledge' conclusion."[6]

Sometimes it is difficult to tell a book review from a critical essay. In fact, some reviews have become so influential, they become part of the critical canon. For example, Edgar Allan Poe articulated his theory of the short story in his 1842 review of Nathaniel Hawthorne's *Twice Told Tales*. However, there are some basic differences between the two forms.[7] Critical essays differ from book reviews in that they are published long after the book has been published and focus on a facet of the book—its theme or thesis, the author's style or perspective, or the ability of an author's premise, method, and research to stand the test of time. A book review, however, is about a recently published book. While it explains what the book is about, it is supposed to focus on a critical evaluation of the content. A scholarly book review generally evaluates the following:

- significance of the thesis or premises
- methods by which the author supported his or her thesis and arguments

- the author's intended purpose
- strengths and weaknesses in argumentation, method, or research
- biases in approach or perspective
- the work in context to other similar works
- the usefulness of the work's demonstration and argument of the thesis
- theoretical issues and topics for further discussion raised by the work
- theoretical assumptions

The process by which reviewers are selected differs among journals. Generally, journal editors seek reviewers who are experts in their field, meaning that they have contributed significantly to the field through scholarly publications. As for the format, reviews range from brief notices to full-length reviews (five hundred to two thousand words). Some journals publish "review essays" that assess the significance of several works linked topically. Moreover, some disciplines have journals devoted specifically to book reviews such as *Contemporary Sociology*, *Envoi: A Review Journal of Medieval Literature*, *Reviews in American History*, and *Reviews in Anthropology*. Furthermore, another format is coming of age on the Internet:

- electronic review journals, such as the *The Medieval Review* (TMR) (www.hti.umich.edu/t/tmr)
- reviews as subscriber e-mails
- electronic review databases, such as the *Anthropology Review Database* (wings.buffalo.edu/ARD)
- discussion networks, such as *H-Net Online: Humanities and Social Sciences* (www.h-net.org/reviews)

While these electronic mediums cannot replace traditional formats, they make book reviews available much faster as well as create a forum for discussion among scholars. Albrecht Classen observes that electronic distribution of reviews "tears down the traditional barriers between reviewers and authors and transforms the reviews into critical statements regarding specific issues first discussed and examined by an author and then thrown into the public sphere. This new media thus provides new channels of communication for the scholarly community which have never before existed in this form."[8]

Objective 3: Locate Scholarly Evaluations of Books.

There is no direct path to finding scholarly book reviews; instead students must take a circuitous route using a several electronic and print indexes. A student needs two things before starting the search. First, bibliographic details of the book, including the publication date. The date determines which tools will most likely include a review. Initial reaction to just-published books often appears in the trades and mainstream press, generally within two months of the book's publication; whereas reviews in the scholarly press—sometimes notoriously slow in bringing out reviews—may appear anywhere from six months to three years. Furthermore, publication dates are important because they will dictate which tools can be used to find them. For example, reviews of Betty Friedan's *The Feminine Mystique*, first published in 1963, cannot be found in *Book Review Index* because it did not begin indexing reviews until 1965.

Scholarly books are assessed, not only by the professional press, but also by the mainstream media. The bulk of these reviews are in trade magazines such as *Booklist, Kirkus, Library Journal, Publisher's Weekly,* and *Choice.* Many of these reviews end up in book review indexes, especially *Book Review Index* and *Book Review Digest,* and general periodical databases. For the most part, these reviews provide a brief description of the book with a dash of evaluative comment. While these reviews come out quickly (especially as compared to the scholarly press), they are of little use to researchers.

Yet, within the mainstream media, there are several review publications that provide lengthy reviews of scholarly books, such as *Times Literary Supplement* (reviews are almost exclusively scholarly), *New York Review of Books, New Republic, Los Angeles Times Book Review,* and, to a lesser extent, *New York Times Book Review.* While some contributors are professors, editors often engage cultural/intellectual essayists and novelists to assess the value of a scholarly work. Hence, their approach and viewpoints often differ from those within the scholarly community, which may explain why many academics are suspicious of mainstream reviewers: they lack background in the area, their assessments lack scholarly rigor, and some are antagonistic to the academic community. On the other hand, many editors of mainstream review publications perceive scholars as pedantic as well as stodgy. As Mark Bauerlein points out, editors prefer books that are "relevant and accessible" and not the "picayune" and "bloviated" books that clog their mailrooms.[9]

When searching print sources such as *Book Review Index*, remind students to search for reviews within twelve to thirty-six months of the book's publication. The earliest reviews usually are from the popular press and trades; later reviews are from the scholarly press.

CLASS ACTIVITIES

One-Hour Sessions

Generally, one-hour sessions do not allow sufficient time to discuss book reviews and their role in the research process. However, when discussing book research, the advantages of book reviews should be mentioned and supplemented with information in handouts, pathfinders, or via a Web tutorial.

Multiple Sessions and Courses

1. Compare and contrast the depth and quality of book reviews published in the trades (e.g., *Publisher's Weekly*), scholarly journals, mainstream press, and Amazon.com. So that students can visualize the differences, display copies of periodicals that contain reviews or reproduce examples on handouts, PowerPoint, or Web pages.
2. Ask students to bring to class a book that they might use for their research. Have them practice evaluating a book by its internal features (see objective 1). Then, ask them to try to locate at least two scholarly reviews of the book.

INSTRUCTOR GUIDES, HANDOUTS, AND EXERCISES

1. Example 8.1: Background Assignment
2. Example 8.2: Researching Book Reviews
3. Example 8.3: Book Review Indexes, A Checklist

Websites on Book Reviews

The following sources provide guidelines on how to write a critical book review:

1. Dalhousie University Libraries, "How to Write a Book Review," www.library.dal.ca/how/bookrev.htm. Provides specific guidelines for reviews in fiction, biography, poetry, and history.
2. Fort Lewis College, John F. Reed Library, "Evaluating Book Sources: A Guide to Writing Your Book Source Evaluation," library.fortlewis.edu/instruct/lib150/bookeval.asp?tcgCache=Go&.
3. Indiana University, Herman B. Wells Library, "How to Write a Thesis Statement," www.indiana.edu/~wts/pamphlets.shtml.
4. University of Alberta, "Writing a Critical Book Review," www.library.ualberta.ca/guides/bookreview/index.cfm. See also, "Book Reviewing Writing Guide," www.uofaweb.ualberta.ca/historyandclassics/bookreviewguide.cfm.
5. University of Waterloo Library, "Writing Book Reviews," www.lib.uwaterloo.ca/libguides/1-12.html.

The following are tutorials for book reviews:

1. Cornell University, Olin and Uris Libraries, "Critically Analyzing Information Sources." www.library.cornell.edu/olinuris/ref/research/skill26.htm#LinkAuthor, and "Book Reviews: A Finding Guide," www.library.cornell.edu/olinuris/ref/bookreviews.html. Includes a brief discussion on the differences between book reviews and literary criticism.
2. Iowa State University Library, "Evaluating Books and Journal Articles Information," www.lib.iastate.edu/commons/old_resources/printeval. Provides a set of questions for evaluating books and articles, covering authorship, publisher, peer review, purpose, and usefulness.
3. Ohio State University Libraries, "Net Tutor: History Research: Finding Book Reviews," liblearn.osu.edu/tutor/history/pg3.html. Includes activity and quiz.
4. Purdue University, "Owl Writing Online Lab: Evaluating Content in the Source," owl.english.purdue.edu/handouts/research

/r_evalsource3.html. Provides indicators on how to ascertain accuracy and objectivity.

5. Skyline College Library, "Finding Evaluations of Books from Book Reviews," www.smccd.net/accounts/skylib/evaluate. html#reviews. Provides a set of questions covering author's intentions and conclusions.

6. University of California, Berkeley, "Finding Book Reviews," www.lib.berkeley.edu/TeachingLib/Guides/BookReviews.html. Covers the basics of locating book reviews.

7. University of Minnesota Libraries, "QuickStudy: Finding Book Reviews," tutorial.lib.umn.edu/infomachine.asp?moduleID=8&l essonID=26. Includes a brief discussion on scholarly vs. popular reviews.

8. University of North Carolina, Chapel Hill, Library, "Evaluating Books" (2004), www.lib.unc.edu/instruct/evaluate. Provides a tutorial and quiz.

9. University of Portsmouth, "Evaluating Books," infoskills.port. ac.uk/useinfo/prelim.htm. Provides brief discussions and questions to help students evaluate the content of a book.

Assessment Tools

1. See examples 8.1 and 8.2 for book review assignments.

2. Review the reviewers. Have students critique two or more reviewers of one book. The critique might include the following questions:

a. How does each reviewer approach the book?

b. What aspect of the book does each focus on?

c. Do they emphasize a summary of the book over critical comment?

d. What are their respective attitudes toward the book?

e. Is each reviewer fair and balanced? Do they balance the book's strengths and weakness?

f. Do the reviewers support their comments using textual evidence or outside sources?

3. Ask students to develop an annotated bibliography of books that they are considering using in their research. Each annotation should address the following:

a. Why are you using this source?

b. Is the source current? If not, why is the information still useful?

c. Are there any scholarly reviews on this book? If so, cite two reviews.

The following websites provide quizzes and exercises:

1. Ohio State University Libraries, "Net Tutor: History Research: Finding Book Reviews," liblearn.osu.edu/tutor/history/pg3.html. Includes activity and quiz.
2. Regis College Library, "Quiz: Evaluating Sources," regisnet. regiscollege.edu/library/infolit/evalquiz2.htm.
3. State University of New York, Oswego Library, "Practice Evaluating Books" (September 6, 2003), www.oswego.edu/library/tutorial/choosbks.html. Very brief quiz on a book's appropriateness for a paper, timeliness, and intended audience.
4. University of North Carolina, Chapel Hill, Library, "Evaluating Books" (2004), www.lib.unc.edu/instruct/evaluate. Provides a tutorial and quiz.

APPENDIX: EXAMPLES

Example 8.1: Background Assignment

The following assignment is to help you prepare for the bibliographical essay assignment, which requires that you select a work published prior to 1900. For each source, explain in one to two fully developed paragraphs why you have chosen a particular book as the best resource for each of the categories. For questions 1 through 4, incorporate comments from at least *two* book reviews. Cite reviews and essays where appropriate. For the author you have selected, choose the best:

1. edition of one creative work or collected works;
2. edition of collected letters *or* memoirs *or* autobiography;
3. biography;

4. literary history related to your author (Literary histories discuss an author's work from a literary/intellectual or sociological/political perspective. For example, one of the best literary histories on the work of Sir Walter Scott is Gary Kelly's *English Fiction of the Romantic Period, 1789–1830* [1989]. Kelly's book was discovered by consulting O'Neill's bibliographical guide, *Literature of the Romantic Period*); and

5. bibliography of secondary sources on the author's work (book-length, article, or chapter; do not include primary or descriptive bibliographies).
Also, please identify:

6. the institution(s) that possesses substantial archives of the author's papers; and

7. a scholarly website devoted to your author. (Describe the focus of the site and explain why it is scholarly.)

Be sure to include a works cited page (MLA style) that includes books and book reviews.

Example 8.2: Researching Book Reviews

1. Locate a scholarly review on the book *Victorian Women Writers and the Woman Question* (1999).

1a. Search the *Humanities Abstracts* (*WilsonWeb*)
   - Reviewer:
   - Journal in which review appears:
   - Date of journal issue:
   - Does the library have this journal?

1b. Search *Academic Search Elite*
   - Reviewer:
   - Journal in which review appears:
   - Date of journal issue:
   - Does the library have this journal?

1c. Compare the results of both databases. Do they both list the same sources?

2. Locate older scholarly reviews for Neil Roberts's *George Eliot: Her Beliefs and Her Art* (1975).

2a. Search the *Book Review Index*
- Reviewer:
- Journal in which review appears:
- Date of journal issue:
- Does the library have this journal?

2b. Search *JSTOR*
- Reviewer:
- Journal in which review appears:
- Date of journal issue:
- Does the library have this journal?

2c. Compare the results of both databases. Do they both list the same sources?

Researching Book Reviews

3. Search for reviews of Andrew Brown's 1993 edition of George Eliot's novel *Romola*.

3a. Search *Humanities Abstracts*
- How many reviews are listed?

3b. Search *Book Review Index*
- How many reviews are listed?

3c. Compare results in both databases. Do both databases list the same reviews?
- *American Libraries*
- *Booklist*
- *Kirkus Reviews*
- *Library Journal*
- *Publisher's Weekly*
- *School Library Journal*

Example 8.3: Book Review Indexes, A Checklist

Book Review Indexes

- *Book Review Digest*, 1905–
- *Book Review Index*, 1965–
- *Canadian Book Review Annual*
- *CBCA Reference* (Canadian)

- *Cumulative Book Review Index*, 1905–1974 (indexes *BRD*, *Saturday Review*, *LJ*, and *Choice*)

General Periodical Indexes

- *Academic Search Premier (EbscoHost)*
- *Academic Search Elite(EbscoHost)*
- *Expanded Academic ASAP*
- *Google Scholar*
- *Lexis/Nexis Academic*
- *OmniFILE (WilsonWeb)*
- *PCI Full Text (Periodicals Content Index) (ProQuest)*, 1770–
- *Palmer's Full Text Online (Times of London)*, 1790–1905
- *Nineteenth-Century Reader's Guide to Periodical Literature*, 1890–1899 (H. W. Wilson)
- *Poole's Index to Periodical Literature*, 1802–1881, supplements, 1888–1906
- *Readers Guide to Periodical Literature (WilsonWeb)*
- *Reader's Guide Retrospective*, 1890–1992

Newspaper Indexes

- *Los Angeles Times (ProQuest Historical Newspapers)*
- *New York Times (ProQuest Historical Newspapers)*
- *New York Times Book Review Index*, 1896–1970
- *TLS Centenary Archive (Times Literary Supplement)*, 1902–1990

Arts and Humanities

- *Africana Book Reviews, 1885–1945: An Index of Books Reviewed in Selected English Language Publications*
- *America History and Life* (ABC-CLIO)
- *American Literary and Drama Reviews: An Index to Late Nineteenth-Century Periodicals, 1880–1900*
- *ATLA Religion Database*
- *Art Full Text (WilsonWeb)*

- *Art Abstracts Retrospective, 1929–1984 (WilsonWeb)*
- *Arts and Humanities Citation Index*
- *Children's Book Review Index, 1975–*
- *Civil War Book Review, 1999–*
- *Combined Retrospective Index to Book Reviews in Scholarly Journals, 1866–1974*
- *Combined Retrospective Index to Book Reviews in Humanities Journals, 1802–1974*
- *Critical Heritage Series* (Routledge and Kagan Paul)
- *Current Contents* (ISI)
- *Current Book Review Citations, 1976–1982* (Citations from Wilson periodical indexes)
- *Early American Periodicals Index to 1850*
- *H-Net Reviews in the Social Sciences and Humanities* (www.h-net. org/reviews)
- *Historical Abstracts* (ABC-CLIO)
- *History of Sub-Saharan Africa: Selected Bibliography of Books and Reviews, 1945–1975*
- *History Reviews of New Books*
- *Index to Book Reviews in England, 1749–1774,* supplement, 1775–1800
- *Humanities Full Text (WilsonWeb)*
- *Index to Black Periodicals*
- *Index to Book Reviews in Historical Periodicals, 1972–1977*
- *Index to Book Reviews in the Humanities, 1960–*
- *Project Muse: Scholarly Journals Online*
- *JSTOR: Scholarly Journal Archive*
- *Literature Online (LION)*
- *Literary Reviews in British Periodicals, 1798–1820: A Bibliography*
- *Literary Reviews in British Periodicals, 1821–1826: A Bibliography*
- *Index to Southeast Asian journals, 1960–1974: A Guide to Articles, Book Reviews, and Composite Works,* supplement, 1975–1979
- *Philosopher's Index*
- *Reviews in American History (JSTOR)*
- *The Romantics Reviewed: Contemporary Reviews of British Romantic Writers, 1793–1824*
- *Women's Studies International*

Social Sciences

- *Book Review Index to Social Science Periodicals*
- *Business Full Text (WilsonWeb)*
- *Econlit (EbscoHost)*
- *Education Full Text (WilsonWeb)*
- *Science Direct (Elsevier)*
- *ERIC*
- *H-Net Reviews in the Social Sciences and Humanities* (www.h-net .org/reviews)
- *Physical Education Index*
- *Reviews in Anthropology*
- *Social Sciences Citation Index*
- *Social Sciences Full Text (WilsonWeb)*
- *Sociological Abstracts*
- *Web of Science* (Thomson ISI)
- *Worldwide Political Science Abstracts*

Science

- *Biological and Agricultural Index (WilsonWeb)*
- *Science Direct* (Elsevier)
- *General Science Full Text (WilsonWeb)*
- *Index to Book Reviews in the Sciences, 1980–1981*
- *Science Citation Index*
- *Web of Science* (Thomson ISI)

The following indexes list books reviews prior to 1980:

- *Africana Book Reviews, 1885–1945: An Index of Books Reviewed in Selected English Language Publications*
- *America History and Life* (ABC-CLIO)
- *American Literary and Drama Reviews: An Index to Late Nineteenth-Century Periodicals, 1880–1900*
- *Combined Retrospective Index to Book Reviews in Scholarly Journals, 1866–1974*
- *Combined Retrospective Index to Book Reviews in Humanities Journals, 1802–1974*

- *Critical Heritage series (Routledge and Kagan)*
- *Current Book Review Citations*, 1976–1982 (Citations from Wilson periodical indexes)
- *Cumulative Book Review Index*, 1905–1974
- *Early American Periodicals Index to 1850*
- *Index to Book Reviews in England*, 1749–1774, supplement, 1775–1800
- *Index to Book Reviews in Historical Periodicals*, 1972–1977
- *Index to Book Reviews in the Humanities*, 1960–
- *JSTOR*
- *Literature Online (LION)*
- *Nineteenth-Century Reader's Guide to Periodical Literature*, 1890–1899 (H. W. Wilson)
- *PCI Full Text (Periodicals Content Index) (ProQuest)*, 1770–
- *Palmer's Full Text Online (Times of London)*, 1790–1905
- *Poole's Index to Periodical Literature*, 1802–1881, supplements, 1888–1906
- *Reader's Guide Retrospective*, 1890–1992
- *The Romantics Reviewed: Contemporary Reviews of British*

NOTES

1. Malcolm J. Ree, "Why Review Books?" *Journal of Educational and Behavioral Statistics* 28, no. 1 (2003): 71.

2. Charles Dickens, *The New Illustrated Oliver Twist*, vol. 16. (New York: Oxford University Press, 1951–1959), 95.

3. Ben MacIntyre, "You May Be Incompetent or Illiterate, but You Can Be a Book Critic Too," *The Times* (London), Features, May 22, 2004, 26.

4. Amy Harmon, "Amazon Glitch Unmasks War of Reviewers," *New York Times*, February 14, 2004.

5. Maxim Gorky, *On Literature: Selected Articles* (Moscow: Foreign Language Publishing House, n.d.), 280.

6. David Henige, "Reviewing, Reviewing," *Journal of Scholarly Publishing* 33, no. 1 (2001): 23–36.

7. Edgar Allan Poe, "Edgar Allan Poe: A Review in Graham's Magazine," in *Hawthorne: The Critical Heritage*, ed. J. Donald Crowley (New York: Barnes and Noble, 1970), 87–94.

8. Albrecht Classen, "Electronic Publishing and the Tenure Clock: Book Reviews and the Electronic Book Review as a New Scholarly Medium of the New Millennium" *LASIE* (June 2000), 56

9. Mark Bauerlein, "Ignore Fast-Track Assessments of Scholarly Books at Your Peril," *Chronicle of Higher Education*, July 19, 2002, B7.

9

SEARCHING THE WEB

Using search engines is thus a contact sport. The user is getting instant feedback and is constantly learning. . . . However, when users pose more comprehensive, complex or varied information requests to search engines, their limitations become apparent.[1]

Goal: To know Internet finding tools and demonstrate how to search them.
Objective 1: Use basic Internet finding tools.
Objective 2: Prepare and execute a Web search query.

A perfect world for a college student is one in which everything on the Internet is free, current, reliable, and easy to find. But as seasoned users of the Internet know, while much of the content is freely accessible, it may not satisfy standards set by professors. Moreover, much of the content-rich websites are not easily accessible; to mine these sources, one needs to be equipped with a variety of search tools.

While many students have grown up using Web search engines, few have had formal training in querying them. Inevitably, students come to college with preconceived notions about Web search engines, such as search engines navigate the entire Web and all retrieve the same results. Furthermore, students approach searching in a rather slap-dash way—punch in a few keywords and hope for the best. However, teaching students to approach a query as a problem to be solved will enable them to rely less on serendipity. Consequently, they will be less inclined to:

- randomly surf or enter keywords higgledly-piggledy or
- become distracted when following a multitude of links

They will be more inclined to have:

- confidence in executing searches and
- patience in examining results

Self-reflection is concomitant with approaching querying as a problem to be solved. That is, students begin to examine their search strategies to discover what works best and what does not. Taking more responsibility for their search strategies enables students to rely less on chance. As students increase their ability to conceptually construct search queries, they will be less likely to see the "the world [as] just a giant bunch of information behind a screen, all of it accessible by keyword."[2]

LEARNING OBJECTIVES AND INSTRUCTOR ACTIVITIES

Objective 1: Use Basic Internet Finding Tools.

Many students begin their research by "googling" the Web. They imagine the Web as a huge database that Google can search all of. While Google is, at present, the largest of the search engines, it overlooks a great deal of information because it is programmed to "crawl" only in certain directions. Thus, to excavate areas untouched by search engines, students need to use a variety of finding tools.

These finding tools can be divided into three groups: search engines, subject directories, and search tools that drill into the "deep Web" (a.k.a., the invisible Web). While the tools within each of these categories can be very effective, none are so good that they can be used in isolation. The tools used are determined by the nature of the topic.

Search Engines   Robots (a.k.a., crawlers) are what drive search engines; they search out and index pages for the engine's database. When a query is entered into a search box, crawlers respond by searching for pages that contain the query's terms. Documents are found in two ways: authors submit their sites or the crawler roams the Web looking for new documents, updating existing documents, and deleting obsolete pages. As Michael K. Bergman explains, "Crawlers work by recording every hypertext link in every page they index. Like crawling ripples propagating across a pond, search-engine crawlers are able to extend their indices further and further from their starting points."[3] Most search engines rank results by relevance, that is, the "best" documents will most likely be listed in the first few pages. Each search engine uses its own proprietary algorithm to rank retrieved results, which is why the same query launched from different search engines will retrieve different results; one may rank a site highly while another does not.

Unfortunately for academic searchers, many of the general search engines are "exhibiting commercial creep," a trend called "paid inclusion" that allows paid-for ads to be embedded in or near relevant search results. Thus, top-ranked search results are cluttered with ads for goods and services. However, because competition for advertising revenues is fierce among search providers, they are highly motivated to seek ways to improve the searching capabilities of their respective search engines.[4]

Academics have found some relief from "commercial creep" in the 2004 release of Google Scholar (scholar.google.com) and Google Book Search (books.google.com), free services provided by Google that enable users to search for academic and peer-reviewed content. In an effort to uncover material beyond the reach of crawlers, Google negotiated with publishers and libraries to link to password-protected content. However, the full text to such content is often unavailable to nonsubscribers. A highlight of the service, however, is its "citation extraction," where Google provides points to links that have cited the original source.[5] The following briefly explains the types of Web search engines.

Standard Search Engines   Standard search engines launch queries across the indexable portion of the Web. Some examples include:

- Ask.com,
- Exalead,
- Google, and
- Yahoo!

Specialized Search Engines   Specialized search engines search a smaller portion of the Web. Chris Sherman and Gary Price refer to these search engines as "focused crawlers [that] limit their roaming to specific sites by editors who supply a list of URLS to be crawled."[6] Examples of topical search engines include:

- Google News (news.google.com) and
- Google U.S. Government Search (www.google.com/ig/usgov)

Some advantages of search engines are:

- a quick response time;
- more specialization than subject directories, that is, they match words found in Web pages indexed by the search engine; and
- currency of retrieved documents better than those in subject directories. However, search engines often overlook new pages because their links have yet to be discovered by the crawlers. Generally, search engines refresh or update databases no more frequently than monthly. Updates include weeding dead URLs (i.e., link rot), downloading the newest version of a page, and adding new pages.

Some disadvantages of search engines include:

- lack of human management
- low precision and recall (for explanation, see chapter 3)
- potential requirement of user's knowledge of constructing complex search queries to locate relevant material
- failure to capture documents in the deep Web (see later this chapter)

Meta–Search Engines   Meta–search engines do not search the Web or generate their own indexes. Instead, a meta–search engine launches a query to multiple search engines simultaneously and integrates the results into a single list. Each meta–search engine has its own list of search engines. For example, the sources for Dogpile include Google, Ask Jeeves, MSN, and Yahoo! Examples of meta–search engines include:

- Dogpile (www.dogpile.com),
- Fazzle (www.fazzle.com),
- Ixquick (www.ixquick.com),
- KartOO (www.kartoo.com),
- Mamma (www.mamma.com),
- Surfwax (www.surfwax.com), and
- Vivisimo (vivisimo.com).[7]

Some advantages of meta–search engines are:

- quick retrieval;
- effectiveness for some esoteric topics;
- grasp of the "big picture" of a topic, that is, a snapshot of what is available;
- potentially highly relevant results due to retrieval the top-ranked sites from each search engine; and
- usefulness when all other search options have failed.

Some disadvantages of meta–search engines are:

- inability to handle complex queries well because of searches across several search engines that have diverse search protocols and
- selective results (meta–search engines generally do not retrieve the total results from each search engine).

New technologies are emerging to improve the coverage and quality of meta–search engine results. One improvement cited by *Search Engine Watch* is that several meta–search engines clearly indicate those results that are sponsored by advertisers.[8] Some search meta–search engines have begun adding other sources other than search engines. For example, additional sources for Mamma.com include Web directories and deep Web content. A few meta–search engines organize their search results into categories (e.g., Vivisimo's Clusty) or into a series of graphic interactive maps (e.g., KartOO).

Subject Directories   Subject directories classify pages and links by subject. Much like the LC classification system, these Web directories organize human knowledge into topical classes, arranged hierarchically from the broadest to the narrowest. However, there is no standard classification system; each directory publisher develops its own scheme. For example, one directory may include a category on "culture," while another omits it.

Unlike the databases built by search engines, directories rely on humans to oversee the selection of, management of, and access to information in their respective "collections." Pages and links included in these collections have been evaluated and annotated by humans, usually volunteers who may be "experts" in the subjects for which they are responsible. Unlike search engines, search queries in subject directories are restricted to words embedded in subject categories, titles, descriptions, and annotations. Some examples of subject directories are:

- Academic Info (www.academicinfo.net),
- BUBL Link (bubl.ac.uk),
- Infomine (infomine.ucr.edu),
- Google Directory (www.google.com/dirhp),
- Librarians' Index to the Internet (lii.org),
- Open Directory Project (dmoz.org),
- Virtual Reference Shelf (Library of Congress) (www.loc.gov/rr/askalib/virtualref.html),
- WWW Virtual Library (vlib.org), and
- Yahoo! (dir.yahoo.com).

Some advantages of subject directories are:

- ease of use;
- browsing capability (benefits those students who have no clue as to where to begin researching a topic);
- low number of sites yielded (prevents students from becoming overwhelmed by too many sites);
- targeting of relevant sites and excludes commercial sites and Internet chatter;

- increased precision, which is often difficult with standard search engines; and
- ability to locate pages and searchable databases "hidden" from search engines.

Some disadvantages of subject directories are:

- uneven quality of content due to many directories' dependence on volunteers to select and evaluate documents;
- slow updates and revisions;
- miniscule content coverage compared to Google and other search engines; and
- difficulty searching for very specific topics, especially those that cross several disciplines (e.g., searching in subject directories for "the attitude of the Catholic Church toward Jews during World War II").

Hybrids and Portals   A hybrid search engine provides a mix of human- and robot-generated results and supplements their search engine results with pages from Web directories. Many well-known commercial search engines, such as Google, are hybrids. For example, Google's directory is powered by the Open Directory Project (dmoz.org), an international Web directory that enlists a core of volunteers to select and evaluate websites.

A Web portal organizes and integrates content, usually focusing on a topic, and distributes it through an array of search tools, resources, directories, services, shopping, e-mail, and chat rooms. Portals can be divided into two groups: general portals, such as Netscape, Google, Yahoo!, and MSN; and specialized portals, such as Yahoo! Finance (finance.yahoo.com), Merck Source (www.mercksource.com), or Law-Guru (www.lawguru.com). Many portals enable users to customize content and toolbars to meet their personal needs, such as listing local weather and traffic conditions. Guides to search engines and directories can be found at:

- Search Engine Watch (searchenginewatch.com) and
- Search Engine Guide (www.searchengineguide.com/searchengines.html).

The following sites provide easy-to-read charts describing the search options of major search engines and subject directories:

- University of California, Berkeley, "Recommended Subject Directories" (www.lib.berkeley.edu/TeachingLib/Guides/Internet/Subj-Directories.html)
- InfoPeople, "Best Search Tools Chart" (www.infopeople.org)

The Deep Web   Google searches several billion Web pages yet ignores or overlooks a plethora of subject matter found deep in the Web. One scientist describes the deep Web this way: imagine the Web being like the ocean, when one throws a huge net across its surface much is captured but much more is lost because of its vast depth.[9]

Awareness of the deep Web first emerged in 1998 when Steve Lawrence and C. Lee Giles concluded that the "engines index only a fraction of the total number of documents on the Web; the coverage of any one engine is significantly limited."[10] In 2000, Michael K. Bergman expanded upon the work of Lawrence and Giles in his white paper, *The Deep Web: Surfacing Hidden Value*. Here are some of his findings:

- Public information on the deep Web is currently 400 to 550 times larger than the commonly defined World Wide Web.
- The deep Web contains nearly 550 billion individual documents, compared to the 1 billion of the surface Web.
- The deep Web is the largest growing category of new information on the Internet.
- Deep Web sites tend to be narrower, with deeper content, than conventional surface sites.
- Total quality content of the deep Web is 1,000 to 2,000 times greater than that of the surface Web.
- Deep Web content is highly relevant to every information need, market, and domain.
- More than half of the deep Web content resides in topic-specific databases.
- A full 95 percent of the deep Web is publicly accessible information—not subject to fees or subscriptions.[11]

Shortly after Bergman's paper, Chris Sherman and Gary Price published *The Invisible Web: Uncovering Information Sources Search Engines Can't See*. Sherman and Price group Web databases into three categories:

1. private, that is content indexed for a specific person (e.g., personal portfolios)
2. real-time/streaming data, that is, data that changes constantly (e.g., stock quotes, weather patterns, and airline schedules)
3. relational databases, that is, databases that allow data to be accessed in a variety of ways[12]

The matter of the deep Web is ignored by standard search engines for two reasons: First, large indexes are costly to build and maintain. Second, search engines are technologically unable to reach some sites either because they are prevented from using them or because they are not "visible" to the search engine. Following are some specific reasons the deep Web is beyond the reach of general search engines:

- They are unable to find pages because there no links pointing to them.
- The webmaster failed to use the "Submit URL" feature to request indexing.
- They are unable to read non-HTML files, such as full-text PDF files, animation, multimedia, and compressed files.
- It is costly to maintain "shortlived" sites that contain real-time data (e.g., stock quotes).
- There are password-protected files.
- Some sites require completion of forms.

Much of the content in the deep Web comprises specialized databases. While search engine crawlers may be able locate an interface or gateway to these databases, they cannot search within them. As Sherman and Price explain, "it's as if [a search engine] has run smack into the entrance of a massive library with securely bolted doors. A crawler may be able to locate and index the library's address, but because the crawler cannot penetrate the gateway, it can't tell you anything about the book, magazines, or other documents it contains."[13] Thus, if a user wishes to search a particular Web database, he or she usually must construct a search query using the tools prescribed by that database. Following are some sites that help users identify subject matter ignored by standard search engines:

- DOAJ: Directory of Open Access Journals (www.doaj.org)
- Infomine: Scholarly Internet Resource Collections (infomine.ucr.edu)
- Internet Scout Project (scout.wisc.edu/index.php)
- PubMed (www.ncbi.nlm.nih.gov/entrez/query.fcgi)
- Scrius: For Scientific Information Only (www.scirus.com/srsapp)
- Science.gov (science.gov)

One effective way of retrieving deep Web databases is to add the word *database* when querying a search engine or subject directory, for example:

- Google search: prisoners/statistics/database
- Yahoo! Directory search: education/database

Librarian Robert J. Lackey's site, "Those Dark Hiding Places: Invisible Web Revealed," (library.rider.edu/scholarly/rlackie/Invisible/Inv_Web.html) provides a gateway that drills into the deep Web. Additional sources that might drill into the deep Web are listed earlier in this chapter under "Specialized Search Engines," "Subject Directories," and "Hybrids and Portals."

Keeping Current To keep abreast of search techniques, search engine assessments, and new deep Web sources, consult the following sources regularly.

Library Weblogs and RSS Feeds These sources help keep instructors current on the latest Web developments. Following are blogs and feeds focusing on Web resources and search technology:

- beSpacific (www.bespacific.com)
- Kept-Up Academic Librarian (keptup.typepad.com/academic)
- Google Librarian (www.googlelibrarian.com/wordpress)
- Information Literacy Land of Confusion (lorenzen.blogspot.com)
- Librarian.net (www.librarian.net)
- Library Stuff (www.librarystuff.net)

- Resource Shelf (www.resourceshelf.com)
- Research Buzz (www.researchbuzz.org/wp)

For additional library blogs, go to Library Weblogs at www.libdex. com/weblogs.html.

Search Engines for News Sources and Blogs   These sources focus on search engine technology and searching:

- Resource Shelf (www.resourceshelf.com)
- ResearchBuzz (www.researchbuzz.com)
- Search Engine News (pandia.com/sew)
- Search Engine Roundtable (www.seroundtable.com)
- Search Engine Watch (searchenginewatch.com)
- Search Engine Watch Blog (blog.searchenginewatch.com)
- Search Engine Showdown (searchengineshowdown.com)
- Search Engine Showdown Blog (searchengineshowdown.com/blog)

General Periodical Databases   Search databases, such as *Academic Search Elite*, for articles related to Internet-searching topics in such periodicals as *Ariadne, Computers in Libraries, eContent, Information Outlook, Information Today, Online, Portal, Searcher,* and *Teacher Librarian.* Supplement these sources by searching in library-related databases, such as *Library Literature and Information Full Text* and *LISA: Library and Information Abstracts,* as well as disciplined-based subscription databases, such as *PsycInfo.*

Web Directories   Consult the home pages of relevant Web directories such as:

- Librarian's Index to the Internet (lii.org)
- Yahoo! Directory (dir.yahoo.com, go to Directory > Computers and Internet > Internet > World Wide Web > Searching the Web > Search Engines and Directories)

Objective 2. Prepare and Execute a Web Search Strategy.

Search engines do not have the capability of conceptually understanding users' search requests. They simply retrieve results that match a search string. For example, they do very well when the search query is unambiguous, such as the name of a company or organization, a quote, or a very esoteric concept. However, simple search-string queries fail to represent abstract concepts or generalized ideas. Documents that best suit the user's needs will not be retrieved because they do not contain the terms used in the search query. As *Business Week* columnists Ben Elgin and John Cady say, "remember, you aren't quizzing a know-it-all. You are looking for words and phrases as they actually appear on a page."[14] For example, a user needing information on brainwashing and religious cults might enter the terms *brainwashing* and *religious* and *cults*. Yet, a key document that discusses mind control and the Branch Davidians would be dropped from the results because it does not contain the search terms used. Hence, until search engines can conceptually grasp what is needed, searchers must know how to construct complex search strategies that will increase the precision of the search results.

The following outlines a sequence of steps that will guide students to construct successful search strategies. Each step describes an action of a series that describes how to formulate a search query, followed with suggestions on evaluating the results against the original search strategy.

Step 1: Articulate the Search Topic.   Students should first try to formulate their research needs as clearly as possible, preferably in the form of a question, phrase, or thesis. For more on framing questions and developing theses, see chapters 1 and 2, respectively. Clearly articulating the search needs at this will help students determine the requisite search tools as well as deconstruct the search statement in a manner suitable for search engines.

Step 2: Know What Is Needed.   Once students become aware of the various search venues offered on the Web (e.g., search engines, Web directories, and invisible Web tools), they will then have a better idea as to what venue best fits their immediate search need. Table 9.1 links search needs with specific Web venues. For more extensive tables that connect research needs to finding tools, visit the following websites:

- Noodle Tools, "Choose the Best Search for Your Information Need," www.noodletools.com/index.html
- SUNY, Albany, "Getting Started: Selecting a Tool for Your Search," www.internettutorials.net/started.html

- University of California, Berkeley, "Recommended Search Strategy: Analyze Your Topic," www.lib.berkeley.edu/TeachingLib/Guides/ Internet/Strategies.html

Step 3: Develop a Logical Search Statement. Once a search tool has been chosen, the next step is to translate the "need" into a logical search statement. *This is important.* If students are unclear in their own minds of what they want, they will translate their lack of clarity to the search engine, which in turn, will respond with confused results. Constructing a logical query is easier if the searcher knows something of the topic being searched as well as the unique "lingo" associated with it. This background knowledge helps students think concretely, thus enabling them to frame a query that will likely increase the precision of the results. For example, a novice searcher may use words and phrases like *drunk* or *drinks too much*, but an authority on the subject will most likely use *alcoholic* or *alcoholism*. The art of searching involves antici-pating what terms will most likely retrieve the best results. To identify terms unique to the topic, encourage students to keep a running list of special terms they run across in their reading. For more about informa-tion about framing research queries, see chapter 1.

Step 4: Construct a Query. This section works best if used in conjunction with the search strategies discussed in chapters 3 and 5. The topic dictates the type of query to formulate. There are four basic search queries: keyword, phrase, Boolean, and proximity. When to use them depends upon two factors: the level of complexity of the query

Table 9.1. Linking Research Need to Web Finding Tools

Research Need	Finding Tool	Example
Browse for ideas or narrow a topic		Web directories, Yahoo!, Google, Open Directory, Infomine, Librarian's Index
Research a topic	General and specialized search engines	Google, Google Scholar, Findlaw, Infomine
Access real-time data (e.g., stocks, weather, or satellite locations)	Search websites and specialized databases	AirNow, NASA Real Time Data, Yahoo! Stock Quotes
Locate or verify a fact or statistic	General and specialized search engines, Web reference sources, searchable websites and databases	Google, U.S. Census Bureau, Internet, public library

and the search syntax of the chosen directory, search engine, or Web database. This section only addresses the former because search syntax among Web interfaces and search tools change frequently. For clear explanations of the search syntax and protocols for various Web search engines and directories, go to UC Berkeley's "Finding Information on the Internet" at www.lib.berkeley.edu/TeachingLib/Guides/Internet/FindInfo.html and InfoPeople Project's "Best Search Tools Chart" at www.infopeople.org/search/chart.html. The following sections outline the type of searches used for simple and complex topics.

Simple Queries   Simple queries look for a *distinct* individual, organization, quote, or esoteric topic. Simple queries do not require synonyms. To execute simple queries, two search strategies are recommended:

1. Use double quotes to keep multiple words together (e.g., "council for responsible genetics" or "human brain project").
2.. Use distinctive terms in the formation of the search string (e.g., hospices / volunteers / California).

Complex Queries   Complex queries are constructed to do four things:

1. They define topics that combine abstract or generalized concepts. These searches require using Boolean operators, for example, (fraud OR scams) AND (web OR internet OR online) AND (stocks OR securities OR bonds).
2. They retrieve words with various spellings, which requires the Boolean OR operator, for example, quechua OR quichua.
3. They eliminate irrelevant pages because some terms also signify brand names, software products, or movies. This requires the use of the Boolean NOT operator or implied Boolean symbol (–). Some examples are Great Expectations NOT (movie OR film OR cinema) and "south beach diet" NOT (cookbooks OR recipes OR amazon).
4. They limit results to specific fields in order to increase relevancy. Depending upon the search engine, limiters may include: title, top-level domain (e.g., edu), URL, geographical area, language, and date.[15]

For additional information on Boolean searching and parenthetical statements, see chapter 3.

Step 5: Know the Search Features of Each Search Engine. Even the most well-thought-out search queries are weakened if they are not executed in accordance with the conventions of the chosen search engine. Users need to be aware that, like subscription databases, Web interfaces are not standardized; each has its own conventions and idiosyncrasies. Hence, users, prior to entering their search (especially complex queries), should determine whether the interface supports basic search features (Boolean and proximity operators, truncation, and nesting) as well as limiters (URL, title, date, etc.). Determining search features usually requires clicking on links like "help," "tips," or "FAQ."

Step 6: Examine the Results. Students tend to be impatient when it comes to examining their search results; many stop reading beyond the first of few hits. They either are satisfied with what they found or assume there is nothing out there on their topic. But as experienced searchers know, initial searches almost always need tinkering. Students should get into the habit of asking the following questions:

- Is this all there is? If so, how do I know this?
- Can I find a few more like these?
- Why did this search retrieve garbage?
- What can I do differently?

Step 7: Modify the Search Strategy. Modifying a search involves altering the original search strategy. Changing a search strategy usually is based on two outcomes:

1. Results are relevant or somewhat relevant. If the results (i.e., the first ten to thirty hits) from the initial search strategy are relevant or somewhat relevant, then one or more the following strategies should be used to improve precision and recall:
   - Identify useful concepts, synonyms, or phrases, and modify the initial search accordingly.
   - Choose the "Search within Results" option (e.g., Google) to narrow the focus of the search.
   - Select a relevant URL and the "related" field limiter to find similar sites, for example, related: vivisimo.com (Google).

2. Search results are irrelevant because of:
   - spelling errors,
   - lack of clarity in search statement,
   - fluff words, or
   - wrong choice of search type, for example, Boolean operators instead of searching as a phrase or with a string of words.

During the search strategy process and its aftermath, students should be taught to reflect upon what worked and what did not and the reasons for those outcomes. By articulating these reflections to the instructor, the instructor can gain insight into how students interact with the search process. These insights enable the instructor to guide students in their roles in the success and failure of constructing search strategies.

Step 8: Evaluate the Trustworthiness of a Site as Well as the Accuracy of Its Content.   This is fully covered in chapter 10.

CLASS ACTIVITIES

The following activities listed can be used in one-hour or multiple sessions. However, in multiple sessions students have the advantage of extended guidance and repetitive practice:

1. Have students evaluate the search results of several Internet search tools. The evaluation might include the types of sites retrieved and the amount of ad content embedded in the results or listed as sponsored ads. For a sample exercise, see example 9.1.
2. To help students see the range and quality of results across a variety of information sources, ask them to research the same topic across an array of electronic tools: OPAC, one or two periodical databases, a standard search engine, and subject directory. Compare and contrast the qualities of each set of results.
3. In their book *Searching and Researching on the Internet and the World Wide Web*, Karen Hartman and Ernest Ackermann provide ample exercises and projects.
4. If pathfinders (print or electronic) are used to supplement an instructional session, incorporate specialized search engines,

Web databases, and directories unique to the subject area. These sources reinforce the fact that "googling" is often inadequate when attempting to capture specialized information.

INSTRUCTOR GUIDES, HANDOUTS, AND EXERCISES

1. Example 9.1: Overview of Internet Search Tools, exercise
2. Example 9.2: Web Directories, exercise

Websites on Search Strategies

The following sites are for use with Google and other search engines. For additional material, search *The Librarians' Guide to Google* (www.googlelibrarian.com).

1. Debbie Flanagan, "Web Search Strategies," www.learnwebskills. com/search/main.html. Includes practice searches.
2. InfoPeople, "Best Search Tools Chart" (April 17, 2004), www.infopeople.org/search/chart.html. Provides an easy-to-read chart describing the search options of major search engines and subject directories.
3. State University of New York, Albany, Library, "Getting Started: Selecting a Tool for Your Search," (November 11, 2004), www. internettutorials.net/started.html. Chart links query types to appropriate search tools. Includes examples.
4. University of California, Berkeley, Library, "Recommended Search Strategy: Analyze your Topic and Search with Peripheral Vision" (August 18, 2004), www.lib.berkeley.edu/TeachingLib/Guides/Internet/Strategies.html and www.lib.berkeley. edu/TeachingLib/Guides/Internet/SearchEngines.html. Provides detailed explanations and examples.

Assessment Tools

Many of the sites listed in this section provide guides and handouts that accompany exercises and tutorials. For additional material, search *The Librarians' Guide to Google* (www.googlelibrarian.com).

1. Steve Bell, "Library and Internet Research Exercise" (August 2003), www.philau.edu/infolit/sba/b122studwksheetfall03.doc. Sections 4 through 6 deal with Web searching.
2. Framingham State College Library, "Quiz 5: Finding Images in the Library and on the Web" (August 18, 2004), www.framingham.edu/wlibrary/instruction/quiz5.htm. Presents a set of seven open-ended questions (and the answers) on locating images.
3. InfoPeople, "Web Search Engines' Special Features," www.infopeople.org/training/past/2003/more_than_google/ex1_se_features.pdf. The purpose of this exercise is to explore the special features of Google and AlltheWeb.
4. Ivy State Tech College Library, "WWW Search Tools Exercise" (October 12, 2004), www.ivytech.edu/library/RTT/ wwwsearch/ exercis4.htm. Exercise asks student to locate information using a variety of search tools.
5. New York University Libraries, "Searching the Web," library.nyu.edu/research/tutorials/www/index.html. Introductory tutorial on Web search tools and search strategies.
6. Purdue University, "CORE: Comprehensive Online Research Education," gemini.lib.purdue.edu/core/default.cfm. Tutorial includes a section on search basics as related to the Internet. Provides a pretest covering various aspects of information literacy.
7. State University of New York, Albany, "Internet Tutorials," library.albany.edu/internet.

The following are tutorials and quizzes for basic and advanced Google searching:

1. Cabrillo College Library, "Using Two Search Engines Finds Good Web Pages on Your Topic," www.topsy.org/Misc/Chapter8Page7.html. Exercise on searching Google, AlltheWeb, and Dogpile. Provides a sample completed assignment.
2. J. Devine and F. Egger-Sider, "Beyond Google: The Invisible Web" (2003), www.lagcc.cuny.edu/library/invisibleweb/default.htm. Tutorial focuses on searching the deep Web.

3. Evanston Public Library, "Advanced Internet Searching," www. evanston.lib.il.us/library/advanced_internet.pdf. Provides detailed tutorial with exercises.

4. Five Colleges of Ohio Library, "Information Literacy Tutorial" (2005), www.denison.edu/collaborations/ohio5/infolit. A collaborative Web-based, interactive information literacy tutorial. Two of the lessons focus on Web research and search techniques.

5. Florida Community College, "Introduction to Internet Research" (2004), faculty.valencia.cc.fl.us/jdelisle/lis2004/index. htm. Detailed tutorial on Web search tools and search strategies. Exercises included.

6. Houghton Mifflin, "Web Research Guide: Internet Quizzes" (2004), www.classzone.com. Provides interactive, multiple-choice quizzes.

7. Leeds University Library, "Intelligent Web Searching," www. leeds.ac.uk/library/documents/workbook/websearch/websearch-workbook.pdf.

8. Greg Notess, "Search Engine Showdown: User's Guide to Web Searching" (2005), searchengineshowdown.com/strat. Provides tutorials on basic and advanced search strategies. Includes exercises Notess has used in his classes

9. Ohio State University, "Net.Tutor," liblearn.osu.edu/tutor. Self-paced Web tutorials on using the Internet for research. Although the site provides overviews of the tutorials to the public, access to full complement of lessons, including assessment instruments, is password protected.[16]

10. Danny Sullivan, "Search Engine Watch: Search Engine Tutorials" (February 27, 2004), searchenginewatch.com/resources/article. php/2156611. Provides brief guides to using search engines discussed in *Search Engine Watch*.

11. State University of New York, Albany, Library. "Internet Tutorials: Using and Searching the Web" (2005), www.internettutorials.net. Provides a full complement of tutorials on using and researching the Web. Includes detailed tutorials on preparing a Web search, selecting search engines and Web directories, and search strategies, including Boolean. See related pages "Second Generation Searching on the Web" (library.albany.edu/internet/

second.html) and "Boolean Searching on the Internet" (library.
albany.edu/internet/boolean.html).

12. University of California, Berkeley, "Beyond General Web Search-
    ing: Advanced Approaches to Finding Information on the Web"
    (March 31, 2003), www.lib.berkeley.edu/TeachingLib/Guides/In-
    ternet/Handouts.html. Covers subject directories, the "invisible
    Web," forums and discussion groups, and the international Web.

13. University of California, Los Angeles College Library, "Road to
    Research," www.sscnet.ucla.edu/library/tutorial.php. Presents a
    set of quizzes that test a student's conceptual understanding of
    research. Includes Web searching.

14. University of South Carolina Library, "Bare Bones 101: A Basic
    Tutorial on Searching the Web" (2004), www.sc.edu/beaufort/li-
    brary/pages/bones/bones.shtml. Provides a full complement of
    lessons on researching the Web, including detailed tutorials on
    specific types of searches such as Boolean, proximity operators,
    and field searching. Provides individual lessons on major search
    engines and meta search engines. Brief assignments conclude
    each lesson.

15. University of Texas System Digital Library, "Tilt" (2004), tilt.lib.
    utsystem.edu. Innovative interactive tutorial on the library and
    Web resources. Includes a module on the thought processes in-
    volved in building search strategies, exercises, and quiz.

16. University of Utah, Health Sciences Library, "Internet Navigator:
    Module 3," www.navigator.utah.edu. This interactive tutorial pro-
    vides two tracks: track 1 focuses on general topics, and track 2 is re-
    stricted to health-related topics. Provides assignments and quizzes.

17. University of Wisconsin, Parkside Library, "Information Literacy
    Tutorial" (2007, October 2004), oldweb.uwp.edu/library/2003/in-
    tro/index.htm.

18. Western Michigan University Library, "Searchpath" (2002), www.
    wmich.edu/library/searchpath. One of the modules focuses on
    Web searching. Includes a quiz.

19. Bright Planet, "Tutorial: Guide to Effective Searching of the Inter-
    net" (2004), www.brightplanet.com/deepcontent/tutorials/search/
    index.asp. Very detailed tutorial in twelve parts, ranging from basic
    to advanced searching. Uses AltaVista for search examples.

APPENDIX: EXAMPLES

Example 9.1: Internet Search Tools, Exercise

For each of the following Internet search tools, enter the keyword search "date rape."

1. General Search Engine: Google.com

1. Number of hits retrieved from the search:
2. Scan the first fifteen sites and answer the following:
   a. Estimated percentage of types of sites
   - self-help:
   - governmental:
   - commercial:
   - nonprofit:
   b. estimated percentage of ad content:

2. Vertical Search Engine: firstgov.gov

1. Number of hits retrieved from the search:
2. Scan the first fifteen sites and answer the following:
   a. Estimated percentage of types of sites
   - self-help:
   - governmental:
   - commercial:
   - nonprofit:
   b. Estimated percentage of ad content:

3. Meta–Search Engine: Mamma.com

1. Number of hits retrieved from the search:
2. Scan the first fifteen sites and answer the following:
   a. Estimated percentage of types of sites
   - self-help:
   - governmental:
   - commercial:
   - nonprofit:
   b. Estimated percentage of ad content:

4. Subject Directories: Open Directory (dmoz.org)

1. Number of hits retrieved from the search:
2. Scan the first fifteen sites and answer the following:
   a. Estimated percentage of types of sites
      • self-help:
      • governmental:
      • commercial:
      • nonprofit:
   b. Estimated percentage of ad content:

Appendix 9.2: Web Directories, Exercise

Compare and contrast results in Google and two Web directories. Enter the keyword search "cosmetic surgery" in each of the following Internet search tools and answer the following.

Google

1. Number of items retrieved:
2. Are there sponsored ads?_____ How many?
3. Estimate the percentage of sites that focus on:
   • services and clinics:
   • information about cosmetic surgery:
   • discussions of the pros and cons of cosmetic surgery:
   • discussions about why people pursue cosmetic surgery:

Open Directory (dmoz.org)

1. Number of items retrieved:
2. Are there sponsored ads?_____ How many?
3. Estimate the percentage of sites that focus on:
   • services and clinics:
   • information about cosmetic surgery:
   • discussions of the pros and cons of cosmetic surgery:
   • discussions about why people pursue cosmetic surgery:

Librarians' Index to the Internet (lii.org) (virtual library)

1. Number of items retrieved:
2. Are there sponsored ads? How many?

3. Estimate the percentage of sites that focus on:
- services and clinics:
- information about cosmetic surgery:
- discussions of the pros and cons of cosmetic surgery:
- discussions about why people pursue cosmetic surgery:

NOTES

1. Bright Planet Corporation, "Why Is Standard Search Alone Inadequate to Meet Real Business Needs?" (2004), www.brightplanet.com.

2. Sue Bowness, "Librarians vs. Technology: Expertise in an Age of Amateur Researchers," *Information Highways* (November/December 2004), www.econtentinstitute.org/issues/table_of_contents.asp.

3. Michael K. Bergman, "White Paper: The Deep Web: Surfacing Hidden Value" (2000), brightplanet.com/technology/deepweb.asp#1.

4. Ben Elgin and John Cady, "Sharpen Your Internet Search," *Business Week*, November 3, 2003, 107.

5. For additional discussions on Google Scholar, see Beth Ashmore and Jill E. Grogg, "Google and OCLC Open Libraries on the Open Web," *Searcher* (November/December 2006): 44–52; and Chris Niehuas, et al., "The Depth and Breadth of Google Scholar: An Empirical Study," *Portal: Libraries and the Academy* 6, no.2 (2006): 127–41.

6. Chris Sherman and Gary Price, *The Invisible Web: Uncovering Information Sources Search Engines Can't See* (Medford, NJ: CyberAge, 2001), 41. See also Gary Price, "Specialized Search Engine FAQs: More Questions, Answers, and Issues," *Searcher* (October 2002): 42.

7. For a more complete list, see Chris Sherman, "Metacrawlers and Metasearch Engines," *Search Engine Watch*, March 23, 2005, searchenginewatch.com/links/article.php/2156241.

8. Greg Jarboe, "Meta Search Engines Are Back," *Search Engine Watch*, December 4, 2003, searchenginewatch.com/searchday/article.php/3109441.

9. Bergman, "White Paper," 1.

10. Steve Lawrence and C. Lee Giles, "Accessibility of Information on the Web," Nature, July 8, 1999, 107.

11. Bergman, "White Paper," 1

12. Sherman and Price, *Invisible Web*, 41.

13. Sherman and Price, *Invisible Web*, 286.

14. Elgin and Cady, "Sharpen Your Internet Search," 107.

15. For additional information on field searching, see Randolph Hock, "The Latest Field Trip: An Update on Field Searching in Web Search Engines," *Online* (September/October 2004): 15–21.

16. This tutorial has been written up in Nancy O'Hanlon, "Net Knowledge: Performance of New College Students on an Internet Skills Proficiency Test," *The Internet and Higher Education* 5, no. 1 (2002): 55–66.

10

EVALUATING WEB SOURCES

One strategy I heard about was that students avoid sites that use a lot of exclamation points.[1]

Goal: To determine the authority and accuracy of websites.
Objective 1: Know how to detect inaccurate information.
Objective 2: Recognize a "possible" trustworthy site.
Objective 3: Investigate and verify ownership of information.
Objective 4: Know major website types that can mislead.

In the early years, the World Wide Web seemed to contain more junk than gems. However, increasingly, this remarkable online environment has been disseminating freely accessible documents invested with authority by scholars, scientists, the government, the medical community, and public policy organizations. Moreover, the Web has proven to be a successful marketplace where opinions, news, and data ignored or suppressed by the mainstream press can be exchanged.

But the very reason that quality information and free exchange of ideas exist in the Web environment is the same reason that it is a breeding ground for useless, fraudulent, and inaccurate information. The

Web is truly "universal, open to all."[2] Because no one entity controls or regulates the Internet, sites can be authored, edited, and published by anyone with technical knowledge of Web design and management. While some sites exert editorial control and facilitate the verification of their content, other sites lack such controls and filters. Thus, the Internet can be described as the "world's largest vanity press."[3]

Several studies have confirmed that undergraduates depend upon the Web for research. For example, the Pew study found that "73 percent of college students use the Internet more than they do the library."[4] These studies also indicate that students are aware that the Web distributes inaccurate information; hence, they do apply some critical standards. The Columbia study found that three quarters of the respondents claim to evaluate the trustworthiness of a source.[5] John Lubans's studies produced a ranked list of factors students use to test the trustworthiness of a site:

1. It is based on a respected print source.
2. It was referred by peers or teachers.
3. The page "ownership" is explicit.
4. The URL has .org or .edu in it.
5. Links on page lead to other sites.
6. The site displays a recent date.
7. There is an e-mail link to the owner.
8. The site looks "professional."[6]

Clearly, these students are evaluating pages but at a very superficial level. While basic indicators, such as ownership and currency of content, are necessary as a preliminary step in ascertaining the reliability of a site, they cannot, in and of themselves, indicate the authenticity of an author's credentials or bias, inaccuracies, and faulty reasoning inherent in the content. A Web document may be authored by an "expert," but even they can make inadvertent errors or deliberately mislead.

Albeit, instructors and librarians warn students that they must go beyond an author's credentials and check whether the document is "objective," "well-researched," and "contains reasonable assumptions." These warnings are often embedded in course syllabi and packaged as Web evaluation "checklists." Well-meaning they may be, but they mean little to novice students. These "warnings" often fall on deaf ears because most undergraduates, especially freshmen and sophomores, lack the analytical skills needed to determine whether content is well researched, biased, or inaccurate. In short, they lack the tools to evaluate beyond the superficial. Thus, beyond determining authorship and currency (that is, if both are clearly stated), students have difficulty dealing with the content-related categories included in a typical checklist. Many librarians agree with the conclusions of Scholz-Crane, Deborah J. Grimes and Carl H. Boening, and Marc Meola that teaching to a simple checklist is not enough.[7] Students need to learn analytical skills that will help them judge the quality of content. As Meola contends, checklists "promote a mechanical and algorithmic way of evaluation that is at odds with the higher-level judgment . . . that [librarians] seek to cultivate as part of critical thinking."[8]

Methods of cultivating students' higher-level thinking skills have been around long before the advent of the Web. And judging from the abundant pedagogical literature on critical thinking prior to 1990, students even then had trouble determining the reliability of information. But those generations of students did not have the pressure of worrying whether a book was reliable. Back then, students trusted the library's collection of scholarly sources, material "filtered" by librarians, bibliographers, and faculty. Nowadays, the Web has added a new dimension to research. Students must expend more intellectual effort in critically assessing the source and content of information. As Vinton G. Cerf observes,

> There are no electronic filters that separate truth from fiction. No cognitive "V-chip" to sort the gold from the lead. We have but one tool to apply: critical thinking. This truth applies as well to all other communication media, not only the Internet. Perhaps the World Wide Web merely forces us to see this more clearly than other media. The stark juxtaposition of valuable and valueless content sets one to thinking.[9]

Thus, while students always have had trouble critiquing research content, the Web makes it imperative that students differentiate the valuable from the valueless. Librarians and faculty need to work independently and collaboratively to teach students how to critically evaluate sources. And students would welcome it. According to the Columbia study, half of the students surveyed never received formal instruction in evaluating electronic sources, and of those, 82 percent believed they could benefit from instruction.[10]

LEARNING OBJECTIVES AND INSTRUCTOR ACTIVITIES

Objective 1. Know How to Detect Inaccurate Information.

This objective focuses on the ability of the student to be aware of personal possible biases, prejudices, or an unwillingness to accept the truth of something that violates his or her belief system. Students should be encouraged to question their motivation to think a certain way. The following are some sample questions:

- Am I being unfair in my view toward X (i.e., idea, opinion, argument, person, or theory)?
- What is my view based on (i.e., personal experience, opinions of friends and family, my fears and insecurities)?
- Am I simplifying X?
- Why do I resist considering other sides of the subject?
- Why do I feel the need to look at X as "right and wrong" or "good and bad"?
- Can I consider that X may be a gray area and that to make an informed decision I must consider all sides of an issue?

While the objective is to help students become healthy skeptics, instructors need to ensure that students do not leave the classroom believing that all persuasive communications are not to be trusted. To prevent such a cynicism from creeping in, D. G. Kiehl and Howard Livingston suggest that teachers introduce a discussion by distinguishing between cynicism and skepticism: "Cynicism involves a contemptuous, pessimistic, disparaging—often bitter—disbelief with no implication of further investigation; skepticism, on the other hand, involves the doubting and questioning of the validity or authenticity of something that purports to be truthful—but with the implication of ongoing probing and testing of evidence."[11]

Objective 2: Recognize a "Possible" Trustworthy Site.

Objective 2 focuses on basic strategies students can use to determine whether a Web source on its surface is trustworthy. Objectives 3 and 4 focus on teaching students investigative strategies that will engage their higher-level thinking skills to determine whether the information *embedded* in the site contains factual errors, fallacies, or nonsequiturs. The evaluation process begins as soon as students encounter a website. They should ask themselves:

- Why is this site here?
- Why do I have free access to this site's information? and
- Why does the publisher want me to see this site?

These questions help students explore the motivation behind the launching of the website. The answers to these questions thus lead students to ask:

- Who funds this source?
- If the site appears to be promoting a product, can I still use the information?
- If the site does not appear to be selling a product, is it trying to promote or advocate something else, such as an ideology or political agenda?
- If the site does not appear to be selling or promoting anything, then what is it? Why is it on the Web? Is an educational institution or government agency funding it? If so, why?

When initially encountering a website, students often evaluate it by limiting the top-level domains (.edu, .org, and .gov), believing (or being told) that cutting out the .com sites will protect them from unreliable sources. However, this is not always the case. Consider the following:

- URLs that end in .org are authored by a variety of groups: public service, nonprofits, and advocacy groups, ranging from the ACLU to hate organizations (e.g., Institute for Historical Review [ihr.org]).
- URLs that end in .com. may not be selling products. For example, public service or nonprofit sites may have a .com domain because their Internet service provider uses it.
- URLs that contain a personal name preceded by a tilde (~)and end in .edu usually signifies a personal website that is housed on a

college server. However, the university may not necessarily stand behind the views contained on the website.

Who Is Behind the Site's Content?   As mentioned, the top-level domain is not always a reliable indicator of who is behind the content of a website. The "who" may involve more than one entity. A website could conceivably have three entities involved: X writes the content; Y sponsors the site; and Z, the webmaster, manages and maintains the site.

Students must learn to determine who sponsors the site. Determining the funding source will often clarify why the site exists as well as alert students that the content may be slanted toward the views of the sponsor. Sponsors can be individuals, advertisers, organizations, the government, or educational institutions. Launching and maintaining a site can be expensive; hence, in doing so, the website's owner may want something in return for the expense. Determining a sponsor may be as easy as clicking on links labeled "About Us," "Mission," "Disclosure," or "Disclaimer." If the identity of the sponsor is unclear, then cut into the URL to the domain name, it may reveal the source of the website. For example, consider the website www.science.smith.edu/departments/Biochem/Biochem_353/MWStds.htm. Truncating to www.science.smith.edu reveals that the site originated from Smith College's Clark Science Center.

Another way of discovering the ownership of a domain name is to consult "whois" databases that supply data on the website, including administrator and technical addresses and server information. These databases include:

- Domain Tools, formerly Whois.sc., (www.domaintools.com),
- GeekTools (www.geektools.com/whois.php), and
- Alexa.com

For additional listings of whois services go to:

- Yahoo! (dir.yahoo.com/Computers_and_Internet/Internet/Directory_Services/Whois)
- Google (www.google.com/Top/Computers/Internet/Domain_Names/Name_Search)

Are They Who They Say They Are? A healthy skeptic will not accept the credentials of an author or sponsor at face value but will go beyond the boundary of the website to verify their credentials. Following are some questions that will help students determine the authenticity of an author:

- Do the site's links tell me anything about this person's credentials?
- Do authoritative sites link to this site? (Students can check by using "link checkers" offered by Google and other search engines.)
- What else has the author written?
- Does the author have a reputation among his or her peers?
- Is the author discussed or cited in relevant subscription databases?
- Is the author listed in standard biographical sources, such as *Who's Who, American Scholars,* or *Contemporary Authors?*
- If membership in professional organizations is listed, is he or she truly a member? (Students can check such sources as *Associations Unlimited, Gateway to Associations, Scholarly Societies Project, IPL Association Directory,* and *All Experts.*)
- Is there an e-mail address where I can communicate with the author?

Once these questions have been answered, students should have a better idea as to what sort of website they are dealing with. The following is a list of the major types:

- personal pages: no affiliation with an entity or institution, such as a university, organization, agency
- commercial pages: home pages of companies, public relations and marketers, advertisements for services and products; may also include studies, surveys, and white papers
- advocacy pages: promotion of social and political agendas
- nonprofit pages: position papers, studies, surveys, and reports issued by professional organizations and public service organizations
- scholarly/educational pages: journal articles, instructional materials, conference proceedings, institutional pages
- government pages: publications from city, county, state, federal, and international agencies

- popular press pages: electronic versions of newspapers and news magazines, alternative news, and weblogs
- archive pages: collections of art, manuscripts, and historical papers
- proprietary pages: password-protected materials, such as commercial databases made available to libraries

Objective 3: Investigate and Verify Ownership of Information.

Websites may not be what they appear to be. They may be reputable, but they may also distort facts, provide erroneous information, omit essential data, or contain illogical argumentation. Students must be taught not to assume that once an author, reporter, institution, or organization has been deemed reliable, the material therein is automatically considered reliable.

Determining the veracity of someone's statements, facts, and conclusions is problematic for undergraduates because they often:

- lack a deep knowledge of the subject they are studying,
- are not trained to identify factual errors and fallacies, or
- may have the attitude that differentiating the valuable from the valueless is not that important.

How can novices begin to evaluate content? How can they know the good from the bad? Successful evaluation begins by becoming a skeptic and asking a few questions that challenge the author's assumptions and factual data:

- Why is this true?
- Why should I believe this author?
- What makes it true?
- Why is it being said?
- What evidence is stated that makes it true?
- Has the claim been tested enough to make it true?

Verifying information proves troublesome for undergraduates because they tend to accept what they read, especially if the source is from a recognized media source (e.g., newspaper or newsmagazine) or a governmental agency. They often have the attitude that if it has been published, it must be true, or if a top governmental official said it, it must be so. Hence, if they do not question the authority of the source, they are vulnerable to accepting erroneous information. The following are basic indicators of accuracy that can help students recognize the need to verify content. Ask students to be aware of and try to ascertain the type of evidence an author uses to support his or her information. For example, Is this historical account backed up by primary sources? Have the findings of X medical study been replicated by subsequent studies? How did the author come up with that statistic?

Anecdotal Evidence   Anecdotal evidence is a claim based on personal observations or a few examples. For instance:

> Violent movies trigger must suicidal tendencies in people because several people committed suicide after watching the Russian roulette scene in *The Deer Hunter*.

Claims backed up by anecdotal evidence are weak because they have not been tested scientifically to show that they are representational of a larger group. To draw firm conclusions about such claims, further investigation based on controlled, quantitative, or empirical studies needs to be conducted.

Sweeping Generalizations   Sweeping generalizations are broad or hasty statements that simplify complex ideas. These types of statements are very common in political rhetoric and are used to stereotype. Statements are signaled by *always*, *all*, *typical*, and *usual*. As Alexandre Dumas said, "All generalizations are dangerous, including this one."[12]

Uncorroborated Evidence   In his article on verification methods, Don Fallis reminds us that Hume "notes that people should pay attention to the 'number of the witnesses' . . . because it is much more likely that one individual will 'deceive or be deceived' than that several individuals will 'deceive or be deceived' in exactly the same way."[13] Hence, several experts who are in agreement about something indicates a consistency and therefore may be an indicator of accuracy. However, those "experts" need to be identified by the author. For example, consider the following statements:

X is true because scientific studies have shown them to be true.
X is true because several historians claim it is true.

While these statements may be true, they have no validity because the author fails to corroborate by citing the studies or the identity of the historians. Failing to sustain statements without corroboration is like the police releasing a suspect on the strength of his alibi alone without independently verifying with others. A word of warning: Many students assume that if the source is footnoted or referenced, it is a "scholarly source." Again, this assumption is not always correct. Consider Ann Coulter's bestselling *Slander: Liberal Lies about the American Right*, which contains over more than seven hundred footnotes, yet many of her statements, as well as footnotes, have been found to be erroneous or deceptive. Another example is Edmund Morris's *Dutch: A Memoir of Ronald Reagan*, which most scholars consider an "intellectual embarrassment" because it blends historical fact with fiction.

Vague Statements   Weak or vague statements are claims that lack specific definitions, concrete explanations, or clear corroboration. For example,

Many Americans use the Internet.

Extreme Statements   Extreme statements run counter to common knowledge, common practice, or scholarly consensus. For example,

Liberals have been wrong about everything in the last half-century.[14]
or,
Saddam Hussein is the single greatest terrorist threat to America.[15]

Currency of Information   In some of the user surveys discussed earlier, students responded that they do check a site for timeliness. But what does "timeliness" imply? Does the date on a website mean that the content has been updated? All of it or just part of it? Or perhaps the content has not been updated but the webmaster updated the site technically.

Facts and Figures   Using facts and figures is a powerful way to support an argument. However, they can also be used to twist information to suit the agenda of the writer. Consequently, students must be taught to be vigilant in using information that can be verified. For example, students may be tempted to use information such as this from a survey discussed on the website ebreastaug.com, a medical marketing firm:

> According to surveyed women that had undergone the breast augmentation procedure, 94% of them said they would recommend the surgery to others. This was an overwhelming response that shows how much breast augmentation procedures have evolved.

While that is an impressive percentage, the website fails to cite the survey that supposedly supports this claim. Unfortunately, many students will accept without question the accuracy of this statement. Unless trained to do so, most students will not think to ask, Who conducted the survey? Was the survey conducted using scientific methods? How can I find the original survey?

Completeness   No one source can provide a full perspective on a topic. Information is inevitably left out. However, many sources leave out information for strategic reasons. Nowhere is this more apparent than sites that advocate ideologies or promote products and services. Often these websites frame issues to suit their purposes, which means omitting views or evidence that supports the "opposition." Students need to be aware that responsible sites include or link to opposing viewpoints or evidence. To counter lopsided coverage, therefore, students should search out and examine several sources that will enable them see the full spectrum of ideas on a topic. Pursuing all sides of an issue also sends a message to students that they are not to omit from their research projects material that does not "fit" their thesis. They, too, must include opposing material and learn to use it to support their own viewpoints. Students should learn to corroborate by locating at least three independent, credible sources that agree with the stated claim, fact, or judgment. These sources must be independent of one another. Otherwise, the documents that are used for verification might be perpetuating the same inaccurate information.

However, in some cases verification can only be successful if the researcher backtracks to the primary source. For example, the popular media continues to perpetuate Al Gore's claim that he invented the Internet. But, if one consults the original source, which was an interview with CNN's Wolf Blitzer, what Gore really said was, "During my service in the United States Congress, I took the initiative in creating the Internet." When taken in context, what he actually meant was that he was instrumental in supporting development of Internet technology.

Objective 4. Know Major Website Types That Can Mislead.

Misinformation   As journalist Carl M. Cannon, points out, "the real computer virus: misinformation."[16] He cites several examples of how Web misinformation spreads to the media and perpetuates itself. For example, in November 1998, the *New York Times* published a series of Chinese translations of Hollywood movies (e.g., *The Crying Game* became *Oh No! My Girlfriend Has a Penis!*) it found on topfive.com, which bills itself as the "best original humor on the Internet." Upon discovering that the titles were spoofs, the paper issued a "red-faced" correction. Yet, other news outlets continued to repeat some of the fake translations, including ABC, CNN, and the *Los Angeles Times*.[17]

Urban Legends, Medical Misinformation, Counterfeit Sites   Hoaxes thrive on the Internet. Online users are especially bombarded by calamitous e-mail warnings alerting them of hostile computer viruses or that the government will shut down the Internet for maintenance or, if a chain letter is not forwarded, something awful will happen. But there are other kinds of hoaxes that students are especially vulnerable to when researching, such as urban legends, counterfeit sites, propaganda, and hate sites. The following briefly explores each type.

Urban legends can circulate for years—remember the "Halloween sadism" tales of the 1950s and 1960s, such as the one about razor blades stuck in apples? While urban legends have been around for centuries, they have proliferated since the advent of e-mail, which can disseminate one of these fictitious stories within hours of its origination. A major reason they proliferate is because they play into the fears of readers who feel the need to warn others. There are several sites that list and monitor urban legends.

While it has yet to be proven that a substantial number of people have been harmed by medical misinformation, these sites can prove problematic for students using them for academic research.[18] Medical hoaxes and misinformation are very real. Encourage students to begin their search with Web directories that will point to sites of established medical associations, such as the American Medical Association, rather than search engines. Students can consult Health on the Net (HON), a nongovernmental agency, at www.hon.ch, which certifies medical and health websites. In addition to applying critical evaluation techniques, students should be aware of "hoaxbuster" sites that monitor medical hoaxes and other fraudulent sites. See later in this chapter, "Fraud Prevention websites."

According to Paul S. Piper in his *Searcher* article, one of the most problematic of the hoax cites are counterfeit sites, which "exemplifies a site pretending to be something it is not, a Trojan horse so to speak. Counterfeit sites disguise themselves as legitimate sites for the purpose of disseminating misinformation."[19] While many of these sites are intended as spoofs, many are malicious. Nevertheless, as Piper points out, these sites can create confusion for searchers. Some are very sophisticated in design and text. Consider the fake site www.gatt.org that mirrors the official page of the World Trade Center. In design they look identical, only the text betrays the difference. The bogus site attempts to undermine the political agenda by replacing official text with subversive text. Less obvious than counterfeit sites are parodies and spoofs, but again, anecdotes from instructors and librarians tell of students falling victim to them. For example, the Onion, Bill Gates?

Propaganda   Ethical persuasion and propaganda both attempt to convince people of the truth as they see it. The difference between the two, however, is that the former uses reasoned argument, and the latter uses manipulation and deception. Not all propaganda is lies; embedded in it are often seeds of truth or half-truths. While the "fact" may be true, the interpretation of the fact is a lie. The purpose of propaganda is to persuade through manipulation, that is, to influence people into buying into a position, opinion, or action. Hitler, for example, seduced his followers through hope and promise. The apparent ease with which many people buy into propaganda is because it manipulates through human weaknesses. For example, advertisers of luxury cars may manipulate potential customers by appealing to their vanity and sense of entitlement.[20] Persuasion can be effected through fear, ignorance, and chauvinism. In the first days following the Oklahoma City bombing, for example, many in the media and the public—reacting from fear, grief, and a need for a quick answer—jumped to the conclusion that Muslim terrorists were the culprits, which turned out to be false.[21] Moreover, people fall victim to lies and distortions because of their propensity to disregard that which runs counter to their beliefs. Liberals and conservatives often fall into this trap—discounting anything that the "other party" asserts.

Students are bombarded with propaganda: in advertising, in the media, and in the political arena. As Sonia Bodi points out, "the problem for our undergraduates is that propaganda provides them with ready-made answers causing them to stereotype which encourages them to avoid thinking, taking a personal stand, or forming their own opinion. The more we read of a particular point of view the more we believe we have an informed opinion."[22] Thus, librarians and instructors must help students learn strategies to prevent them from accepting blindly what they read and to suspend judgment until they can weigh the evidence. In his book on the goals of higher education, Patrick Nuttgens comments, "the mark of an educated person is that issues are no longer simple, that they are not black or white, that the truth lies somewhere in the middle, and that there is no escape from the responsibility of knowing one's mind and making one's own decisions."[23]

If ethical persuasion and propaganda seek to influence people's beliefs, how can students differentiate between them? First, make students aware of the core differences between those that persuade honestly as opposed to those whose aim is to persuade through lies, distortions, and misrepresentations. The following describes some of these core differences.[24]

Characteristics of a Propagandist

- Ignores the "other side" by omitting, distorting, or glossing over evidence
- Encourages thinking in black and white by reducing complex issues to simple explanations or solutions
- Appeals to the emotions more than the intellect

Characteristics of an Ethical Persuader

- Respects the audience and their right to differ
- Views the audience as partners in a honest conversation about ideas
- Does not ignore the other side; recognizes opposing claims
- Claims a solution based on logical reasoning and argument
- Appeals to evidence, rather than emotion, to support position

This list will make students aware that there are differences in how information is constructed as well as help to dispel the widely held belief that propaganda is something other countries do.[25] Thus, enlightened students can begin testing claims, arguments, and so-called factual statements by first knowing the motivation underlying their personal belief system (discussed in objective 1); determining the trustworthiness of a website (discussed in objective 2); and applying techniques of verification (discussed in objective 3).

CLASS ACTIVITIES

Teaching students how to question evidence, resolve conflicting statements, detect fraudulent information, and evaluate the quality of sources challenges instructors because successful outcomes depend upon cultivating students' higher thinking. Yet, teaching evaluative techniques can be fulfilling and challenging for instructors. The content is an attention grabber for students, unlike the tedium of some research skills. And, several research skills can be woven into the instructional session. For example, the following illustrates how students can learn to verify facts and statements by using their search skills and knowledge of research sources.

1. Session Strategy: Did Al Gore really claim that he invented the Internet? Have students research the story that Al Gore claimed to have invented the Internet. Begin by asking them to look at several sources that repeat the story. Most general periodical databases will list several articles including Joshua Green's article in the *Atlantic Monthly*. Then ask students to question the veracity of the statement, Did Al Gore really say this? If so, where did the statement originate?[26]

   One strategy to help students begin their search for the original source is to enter a Google search (e.g., gore/internet/invent). Near the top of the results is a page from snopes.com, which states that the story is a distortion of remarks Gore made during an interview with CNN's Wolf Blitzer on March 9, 1999.[27] At this point, students should not accept this as verification. They now must locate the actual transcript of the interview, which can be located in Lexis/Nexis. Reading the transcript verifies that Gore's remarks were taken out of context.

This exercise enables students to become aware of how information can be distorted, how the media repeats distortions without verification, and how they can use their searching skills to verify information.

2. Assign students to evaluate a specific unreliable website, and then ask them to research the website in Lexis/Nexis to see if news reports cite this source. A good example to use is www.city-data.com/city/ Santa-Fe-New-Mexico.html. The site provides facts and figures for the city of Santa Fe but fails to document the information other than stating that it was gathered from multiple governmental and commercial entities. In fact, the disclaimer advises users to use at their own risk because the provider does not guarantee accuracy. Yet, when the domain (www.city-data.com) is searched in Lexis/Nexis using the full-text field, several articles cite data from the site.

3. Have students compare a website with an article they are using for their research project. Ask them to determine whether the facts vary between the site and the article.[28]

4. As a small-group activity, have students critique an evaluation written by a student. Provide a set of questions as guide. See examples 10. and 10.2 for sample student evaluations and questions.

Increasingly, primary and secondary material is being made available on the Internet. Students should know how to recognize evidence originating from these two kinds of sources. See example 10.3 for a brief discussion of primary versus secondary sources as well as some student activities.

These sources provide content to develop lectures, conduct demonstrations and discussions, and design exercises:

Block, Marylaine. "Gullible's Travels." *Library Journal* (Net Connect) 127 (Spring 2002): 12–14. Discusses how to make students aware of covert propaganda sites, such as the Institute for Historical Review (www.ihr.org), which attempts to legitimize the Holocaust denial movement via "the trappings of academic argument." See also Borrowman's article on how to use this site to teach Web evaluation.

Bodi, Sonia. "Scholarship or Propaganda: How Can Librarians Help Undergraduates Tell the Difference?" *Journal of Academic Librarianship* 21

(1995): 21–25. Describes a series of instructional sessions that teach students the differences between scholarship and propaganda. Students use a set of indicators for scholarship and propaganda as a guide in analyzing the assigned articles.

Borrowman, Shane. "Critical Surfing: Holocaust Denial and Credibility on the Web." *College Teaching* 47, no. 2 (1999): 44–48. Demonstrates how a combination of academic credentials and Internet technology can construct credible arguments to support hate and bigotry. To illustrate, Borrowman discusses how Dr. Arthur Butz, associate professor at Northwestern, "presents himself as a scholar engaged in the pursuit of truth, a truth which stands in opposition to the accepted version of the history of the Holocaust." The author also discusses Butz' ties with the Institute for Historical Review (www.ihr.org). See also Bodi's article.

Browne, M. Neil, et al. "The Importance of Critical Thinking for Student Use of the Internet." *College Student Journal* 34 (2000): 391–98. To illustrate the existence of websites that contain conflicting information, the authors compare two sites on lowering the legal drinking age.

Connor-Greene, Patricia A., and Dan J. Greene. "Science or Snake Oil? Teaching Critical Evaluation of 'Research' Reports on the Internet." *Computers in Teaching* 29, no. 4 (2002): 321–24. Describes a class exercise in which students examined an article on the dangers of aspartame and recorded their reactions to the article. Then, they broke into small groups and addressed a series of questions and reconvened to discuss as a class.

Drobnicki, John A., and Richard Asaro. "Historical Fabrications on the Internet: Recognition, Evaluation, and Use." *Reference Librarian* 74 (2001): 121–64. Discusses several examples of websites that provide false historical information ranging from hoaxes, spoofs, counterfeit sites, and conspiracy theories.

Ensman, Richard. "The Scoop on Internet Hoaxes." *Poptronics* (February 2000): PS3–PS5. Identifies specific types of Internet hoaxes: good-times hoaxes, pen pals, money scams, computer viruses, freebies, danger alerts, household poisons, heart throbbers, and citizen action. Follows up with quick tips on how to recognize these types of hoaxes.

Gibson, S., and Joanne Tranter. "Internet Information: The Whole Truth?" *Canadian Social Studies* 34, no. 4 (2000): 77–80. Discusses a brainstorming exercise that helps students think critically about Internet sites.

Hiebert, Eldon. "Public Relations and Propaganda in Framing the Iraq War: A Preliminary Review." *Public Relations Review* 29, no. 3 (2003): 243–55. Hiebert discusses the Internet and its role in subverting the government propaganda machine.

Lorenzen, Michael. "Hoax or Just Strange? A Web Evaluation Exercise." lorenzen.blogspot.com/2006/10/hoax-or-just-strange-web-evaluation.html. Discusses a class exercise on detecting hoax sites.

Lynch, Darlene, et al. "Critical Thinking and the Web." *Journal of Social Work Education* 37, no. 2 (2001): 381–86. Recognizes the importance of social workers learning to critique websites for course work, working with clients, and grant writing. Covers specific techniques in determining public service/nonprofit sites from commercial and research sites from fraudulent ones, detecting deceptive mission statements, and recognizing pseudoscience, scams, and hoaxes. Includes pedagogical examples useful for social and behavioral disciplines.

Meola, Marc. "Chucking the Checklist: A Contextual Approach to Teaching Undergraduates Web-Site Evaluation." *Portal: Libraries and the Academy* 4, no. 3 (2004): 331–44. Provides explanations and examples of three methods of approaching Web evaluation contextually, promoting/explaining peer-review sources, comparisons, and corroboration.

Miller, Nora. "Anti-Spin: Using Internet Resources to Unwind Political Claims." *ETC: A Review of General Semantics* 62 (2005): 75–89. Annotates several websites that assess the claims made by politicians.

Olson, John A. "How to Encourage Students in a Library Instruction Session to Use Critical and Creative Thinking Skills." *Research Strategies* 16 (1998): 309–14. Explains how he incorporates creative thinking processes and Berry K. Breyer's elements of critical thinking (disposition, criteria, argument, reasoning, and point of view) into a one-shot session. Olson also suggests several classroom techniques, such as the Socratic method, to motivate students to think critically about the information-seeking process.

Piper, Paul S. "Better Read That Again: Web Hoaxes and Misinformation." *Searcher* (September 2000): 40–49. Delineates several categories and examples of hoaxes: counterfeit, parodies and spoofs, fictitious, and subject-specific sites.

Scott, Robert Ian. "Politics, Advertising, and Excuses: Why Do We Lie?" *ETC* 61, no. 2 (2004): 187–95. Provides examples of how propaganda works in the press and in advertising.

Tate, Marsha Ann. "Looking for Laura Secord on the Web: Using a Famous Figure from the War of 1812 as a Model for Evaluating Historical Web Sites." *History Teacher* 38 no.2 (2005): 225–40. Assesses how Secord's deeds are depicted on the Web and based on twelve websites devoted to Secord. Tate had difficulty in establishing the identity of the author and his or her credentials. She demonstrates how these sites provide widely varying accounts of Secord's deeds. Moreover, these sites tend to present a "black and white" picture of Secord, thus avoiding historical surrounding Secord's historical legacy.

The following lists articles that focus on the evaluation of medical websites:[29]

Kahana, Alon, and Gottlieb, Justin L. "Ophthalmalogy on the Internet: What Do Our Patients Find?" 122, no. 3 (2004): 382–84. Good resource supplementing a lecture on evaluation of medical websites. Studied whether the results of searches on macular degeneration performed across several search engines are biased toward commercial sites. Concludes that the results of some search engines are "heavily tilted" toward commercial sponsors while others emphasized nonprofit and educational sites.

Lissman, Thomas L., and James K. Boehnlein. "A Critical Review of Internet Information about Depression." *Psychiatric Services* 52 (2001): 1046–50. Examined the results performed on ten general search engines of a treatment of depression. Concludes that the overall content was of poor quality. Commercial sites appeared much more frequently in the top-ranked results.

Murphy, Rebecca, et al. "Evaluation of Web-based Information." *International Journal of Eating Disorders* 35 (2004): 145–54. A good source of information for instructors who wish to use medical websites to teach Web evaluation. This study critiqued fifteen commonly accessed websites related to eating disorders. Concludes that the overall quality of the sites are poor.

Randal, Judith. "Study Evaluates Information on Breast Cancer Web Sites." *Journal of the National Cancer Institute* 96, no. 6 (2004): 430. Reports on a recent study that addressed the question "Does the Internet tell women what they need to know about screening mammography?" The study evaluated twenty-seven websites and concluded that many of these sites provided misleading information on the benefits and risks of screening.[30]

Ziel, Harry K. "How to Evaluate New Medical Discoveries." *Skeptic* 7, no. 2 (1999): 40–42. Provides a succinct comparative explanation of how reliable and unreliable scientific information is transmitted in print and on the Internet.

INSTRUCTIONAL GUIDES, HANDOUTS, AND EXERCISES

1. Examples 10.1–10.2: Student Web evaluations
2. Example 10.3: Primary and Secondary Sources

Websites on Evaluation Checklists

1. Jan Alexander and Marsha Tate, "Widener University Evaluating Web Resources" (July 30, 2002), www-personal.umich. edu/~pfa/pro/courses/EvalPtEd.pdf. Provides sample websites and a PowerPoint presentation on evaluating websites. Includes separate checklists for business, personal, news, informational, and advocacy.

2. Johns Hopkins University Libraries, "Evaluating Information Found on the Internet," www.library.jhu.edu/researchhelp/general/evaluating/index.html. Provides a special section on detecting counterfeit sites.

3. New Mexico State University, "The Good, Bad, and the Ugly, or, Why It's a Good Idea to Evaluate Web Sources," lib.nmsu.edu/instruction/ eval.html. A set of examples accompany the evaluative criteria.

4. Pace University Library, "Web Site Evaluation Worksheet" (May 2002), www.pace.edu/library/instruct/webevalworksheet.htm. The worksheet comprises fifteen questions that students answer as they evaluate a particular website.

5. Lake Sumter Community College Library, "Evaluating Library Resources" (2005), www.lscc.edu/library/guides/evallib.htm. Divides evaluative criteria into three area: preliminary, content analysis, and scholarship and propaganda. Draws upon the work developed by UC Berkeley professor Eileen Grambrill.

6. University of California, Berkeley, Library, "Evaluating Web Pages: Techniques to Apply and Questions to Ask" (July 27, 2006), www. lib.berkeley.edu/TeachingLib/Guides/Internet/Evaluate.html.

7. Kathy Schrock, "Critical Evaluation of a Web Site Worksheet" (2003), school.discovery.com/schrockguide/evalhigh.html. Detailed worksheet appropriate for incoming freshmen. See also Wartburg College Library, "Web Worksheet," www.wartburg. edu/library/vesa.html. Worksheet that uses a point system. Appropriate for incoming freshman.

8. University of Mississippi Libraries, "Evaluating Web Sites," www. olemiss.edu/depts/general_library/files/bi/levelthree/eval_web. htm. Presents a set of questions for students to consider when evaluating websites.

Links to Examples of Websites for Evaluation Demonstrations These sites are useful in identifying websites for assignments and in-class group activities. For example, assign a small group a website, and have them apply evaluative criteria and report the results to the class. See also "Fraud Prevention Websites."

1. Annenberg Political Fact Check, www.factcheck.org. A project of the Annenberg Public Policy Center of the University of Pennsylvania, this site's mission is to "monitor the factual accuracy of what is said by major political players in the form of TV ads, debates, speeches, interviews, and news releases."
2. Bowling Green State University Libraries, "Web Wizard: Your Guide to Becoming an Effective Web Searcher" (2005), www.bgsu.edu/colleges/library/infosrv/lue/webwizard/evaluate.html. Provides sample websites for students to practice their critical thinking skills.
3. Consumer Health, "Web Site Evaluation Checklist," www.personal.umich.edu/~pfa/pro/courses/EvalPtEd.pdf.
4. "Spinsanity: Countering Rhetoric with Reason," www.spinsanity. org. Deconstructs dishonest statements made by politicians, pundits, and journalists and debunks myths spread by the media. The site is no longer updated.
5. Virginia Tech University Libraries, "Bibliography on Evaluating Web Information" (August 13, 2004), www.lib.vt.edu/help/instruct/evaluate/evalbiblio.html#forms. Includes lists of websites covering evaluation forms, examples of websites, samples of hoax and humorous sites, and bibliography of sources discussing Web evaluation.
6. University of North Carolina, Asheville, Ramsey Library, "In Class Small Group Assignment," bullpup.lib.unca.edu/library/infolit/as_evalweb.html. Provides a list of four websites.
7. Wake Forest University Library, "Evaluating Web Resources," zsr.wfu.edu/research/guides/web/eval.html. Provides a list of sixteen sites students can evaluate.

Websites on Reasoning and Logical Fallacies The sites and sources listed below provide concise explanations of reasoning and logical fallacies.

1. Committee for the Scientific Investigation of Claims of the Paranormal, "A Field Guide to Critical Thinking," www.csicop. org/si/9012/critical-thinking.html.
2. Humboldt State University, "Argumentation and Critical Thinking Tutorial," www.humboldt.edu/~act/HTML. Includes multiple-choice, true/false, and short-answer tests.
3. Metropolitan Community College, "A Tutorial in Critical Reasoning" (February 20, 2001), commhum.mccneb.edu/argument/summary.htm. Includes short exercises.
4. Princeton University, "Avoiding Common Errors in Logic and Reasoning" (1999), webware.princeton.edu/sites/writing/handouts/logic&reason.pdf.
5. San Jose State University, "Critical Thinking Web Page," www.sjsu.edu/depts/itl/graphics/main.html. Provides tutorials, examples, and exercises.
6. Peter Suber, "Real World Reasoning" (1998), www.earlham.edu/~peters/courses/inflogic/inflinks.htm. Provides his students with numerous links on reasoning, fallacies, and critical thinking.

Websites on Fraud Prevention and Fact Checking   The websites below track fraudulent websites. For additional sites, go to Google Directory at www.google.com/dirhp?hl=en and point to Reference > Education > Instructional Technology > Evaluation > Web Site Evaluation > Hoax Sites.

1. Center for Disease Control, "Health Related Hoaxes and Rumors" www.cdc.gov/hoax_rumors.htm
2. "Don't Spread That Hoax," www.nonprofit.net/hoax
3. Hoax Slayer, www.hoax-slayer.com
4. Museum of Hoaxes, www.museumofhoaxes.com
5. Quackwatch, www.quackwatch.com
6. ScamBusters, www.scambusters.org/index.html
7. Snopes.com
8. U.S. Department of Energy, "Computer Incident Advisory Capability (CIAC)" (October 4, 2004), hoaxbusters.ciac.org
9. U.S. Federal Trade Commission, "Consumer Information" (November 8, 2004), www.ftc.gov/bcp/menu-internet.htm (See also

the FTC's publication on diploma mills at www.ftc.gov/bcp/edu/pubs/consumer/alerts/alt149.htm.)

10. U.S. Food and Drug Administration, "How to Spot Health Fraud" (October 8, 1999), www.fda.gov/fdac/features/1999/699_fraud.html

11. U.S. National Library of Medicine, "Health Fraud" (November 4, 2004), www.nlm.nih.gov/medlineplus/healthfraud.html

Assessment Tools

1. Acadia University, Vaughn Memorial Library, "Credible Sources Count," library.acadiau.ca/tutorials/webevaluation. Basic interactive tutorial.

2. Anne Anderson, Northern Virginia Community College, "Evaluating Web Sites," www.nvcc.edu/alexandria/library/instruction/esl/evaluatewebsites.htm. Exercise asks student to apply Web evaluation skills to a selection of websites.

3. P. F. Anderson et al., "Web Site Evaluation Checklist" (1998), www.personal.umich.edu/~pfa/pro/courses/Web. Checklist of evaluative indicators in chart form (PDF). Includes instructions on how to score each indicator.

4. Ballard, Spahr, Andrews, and Ingersoll, LLP. "The Virtual Chase: Teaching Legal Professionals How to Do Research" (November 29, 2004), www.virtualchase.com/quality/index.html.

5. Colorado State University Libraries, "Evaluating Web Sites," lib.colostate.edu/tutorials/webeval_info.html. Provides an interactive tutorial.

6. Duke University Libraries, "Evaluating Web Pages." www.lib.duke.edu/libguide/evaluating_web.htm. Graphic tutorial covering basic evaluative indicators (e.g., authority, currency, bias, etc.).

7. Intute Virtual Training Suite, "Internet Detective: Wise Up to the Web," www.vts.intute.ac.uk/detective/index.html. Free basic tutorial developed for United Kingdom universities and colleges.

8. Ithaca University Library, "ICYou See: T Is of a Guide to Critical Thinking about What You See on the Web," www.ithaca.edu/library/training/think.html. Includes exercises.

9. Ohio State University Libraries. "Evaluating Web Sites," liblearn.osu.edu/tutor/les1. Tutorial includes examples and exercises.

10. Purdue University Libraries, "Evaluating Web Sites: A Tutorial," www.lib.purdue.edu/ugrl/staff/sharkey/interneteval/index.html. A set of worksheets accompanies the tutorial.

11. State University of New York, Albany, Library. "Evaluating Internet Sites 101," library.albany.edu/usered/webeval. Introductory tutorial.

12. University of Alaska, Fairbanks, Rasmuson Library, "Evaluating Databases vs. Internet Searches" (2005), www.uaf.edu/library/instruction/handouts/Info_Resources.html. Interactive exercise that includes Web evaluation and Internet and database searching.

13. University of California, Berkeley, "Evaluating Web Sites: Techniques to Apply and Questions to Ask," www.lib.berkeley.edu/TeachingLib/Guides/Internet/Evaluate.html. Provides in-depth guidance in evaluating websites.

14. University of California, Irvine, Science Library, "Evaluating Web Sites" sun3.lib.uci.edu/~sclancy/search/exercise02.htm. Exercise asks students to compare a list of websites that differ in subject, purpose, bias, and design.

15. University of California, Los Angeles Libraries, "Hoax? Scholarly Research? Personal Opinion? You Decide!" (2000), www.library.ucla.edu/libraries/college/help/hoax/index.htm. Brief exercise testing six indicators: authority, accuracy, advocacy, and objectivity. Students evaluate a set of websites. Appropriate as an in-class activity.

16. University of Massachusetts, "Evaluating Web Sources Exercise," www.umassd.edu/specialprograms/info_lit/evaluating_exercise.html. Students evaluate sample websites. Accompanying each site is a set of questions to guide students. Appropriate as an in-class activity.

17. University of Mississippi Libraries, "Evaluating the Web Tutorial," www.olemiss.edu/depts/general_library/files/bi/leveltwo/evaluating.htm. Tutorials include exercises.

18. University of North Carolina, Chapel Hill, Library, "Evaluating Websites" (2004), www.lib.unc.edu/instruct/evaluate. Provides a tutorial and quiz.

19. University of Utah, Health Sciences Library, "Internet Navigator: Modules 3," www-navigator.utah.edu. This interactive tutorial includes assignments and quizzes.

20. Widener University, Wolfgram Memorial Library, www3.widener.edu/Academics/Libraries/86. Provides tutorial and exercise.

APPENDIX: EXAMPLES

Example 10.1: Student Web Evaluation No. 1

Website: Heart of American Northwest (www.heartofamericanorthwest. org/index_page.html)

The website that I have evaluated is Heart of American Northwest. This website is authored by HOANW, an organization that provides "highly credible information" about the waste being dumped at the Hanford Nuclear Reservation in the state of Washington. This organization does not seem to have a political agenda; they only want to inform people about the history and future of the Hanford waste site. The site is very well documented with verifiable resources. The information provided by this website is fairly recent.

Suggested questions for the class to consider:

1. This site's mission statement claims it uses "highly credible information" to advance it purpose of improving the quality of life in Washington. Where is this information cited in the website? Is it credible?
2. The site claims to provide an historical overview of the Hanford Nuclear Reservation. How do you know that the statements, facts, and statistics are accurate? Do the authors source the information?
3. The student claims that HOANW does not have a political agenda, that it is not advocating and supporting a cause. Is he or she correct in this assertion? Is the purpose of this organization solely to "inform people about the history and future of this waste site"?
4. The site is highly critical of the U.S. Department of Energy's role in the dumping of waste at Hanford. Does the site present the view of the issue from the standpoint of the Department of Energy?

Example 10.2: Student Web Evaluation No. 2

Website: U.S. Environmental Protective Agency (EPA) (www.epa.gov)

EPA is an informational website put forth by the U.S. government. This website would be acceptable to my instructor because it consists of government documents. This site is documented with many verifiable sources. The EPA's goal is to protect the environment. I would say this site has no bias because it contains straight facts from the government. A lot of the information is over five years old. So it would not be helpful because many advances have occurred in various fields like mercury poisoning.

Suggested questions for the class to consider:

1. The student makes the vague statement that the EPA site provides "many verifiable sources." How does the student know they are "verifiable?"

2. This student states that this site contains no bias because it provides "straight facts from the government." What does the student mean by "straight facts?" Is everything published by the U.S. government objective?

3. This student, like many, automatically assumes that all documents issued by the government are objective and truthful. Of course, this is not always the case. Depending on the topic, government documents often reflect the policies of the administration in power. Consider the EPA's stance on the impact of mercury emissions on children's health. In spring 2005 a Lexis/Nexis search revealed that several newspapers reported that scientists, physicians, and the Government Accountability Office (GAO) criticized as flawed the EPA's analysis of the affect of mercury emissions on children. Moreover, the EPA suppressed its own study on mercury emissions it commissioned Harvard to conduct. This study contradicted the EPA's conclusions that mercury emissions from power plants are not a threat to public health.

4. The student indicates that the site's content contains dated material and thus would not be helpful in researching the mercury emissions. While current information is vital, how could the older information assist a researcher?

Example 10.3: Primary and Secondary Sources

Primary sources provide the raw material for research. They range from firsthand accounts of a historical event to creative works to scientific articles reporting research results. Primary sources allow students to study evidence firsthand without being influenced by the interpretations or analyses of others. Examples of primary sources include the following:

- testimony or direct evidence
- court reports
- diaries, autobiographies, letters
- creative works (e.g., musical scores, plays, and original art)
- scientific articles reporting original research
- birth certificate or driver's license

Secondary sources interpret, evaluate, or analyze the content of primary sources. Secondary documents provide a frame of reference for students and help them become aware of how others have interpreted the topic or event. Examples of secondary sources include the following:

- critical essay on Shakespeare's play *Romeo and Juliet*
- historian's interpretation of an event situated in the past
- textbook on biology

The following are sources that further define primary and secondary sources and provide search strategies in locating these documents:

1. California State University, Monterey Bay, "Primary Sources and Secondary Sources," library.csumb.edu/instruction/howto/primary.php. Provides chart that identifies types of primary/secondary sources and the search tools needed to locate them.
2. Library of Congress, "Using Primary Sources in the Classroom," memory.loc.gov/learn/lessons/psources/source.html. Provides a lesson plan and suggested activities for using primary source materials with a historical context. Also includes graphic examples of primary sources: artifacts, letters, photographs, manuscripts, and so on.
3. Iowa State University Library, "Defining and Finding Primary Sources," www.lib.iastate.edu/commons/resources/primary/primary.html. Discussion focuses on historical research.
4. Ohio Historical Society, "Using Primary Source Documents in the Classroom," www.ohiohistory.org/resource/teachers/primary.

html#definitions. Includes lesson plans that focus on evaluating primary documents.

5. University of California, Berkeley, Library, "Library Research; Finding Primary Sources," www.lib.berkeley.edu/TeachingLib/ Guides/PrimarySources.html#primary. Provides a chart that breaks down types of primary sources and suggestions for ways to locate a particular type of primary document.

6. Yale University, "Primary Sources," www.library.yale.edu/instruc-tion/primsource.html. Provides detailed discussion of the catego-ries of primary sources, such as published texts, manuscripts, and visual materials.

7. University of Texas, "Primary vs. Secondary Sources," www.lib. utexas.edu/services/instruction/ faculty/PriSec.html. An assign-ment that requires students to identify primary and secondary sources related to James Joyce's *Ulysses*.

NOTES

1. John Lubans, "When Kids Hit the Surf: What Do Kids Really Do on the Internet?" (1999), www.lubans.org/nynma.html.

2. Tim Berners-Lee, "The Internet's Creator Looks to the Next Evolution," *Electronic Design*, September 13, 2004, 90.

3. Joshua Green, "Playing Dirty," *Atlantic Monthly* (June 2004): 321.

4. Steve Jones, "Internet Goes to College: How Students Are Living in the Future with Today's Technology," *Pew Internet and American Life Proj-ect*, September 15, 2002, www.pewinternet.org/pdfs/PIP_College_Report.pdf. Other studies include: OCLC, "White Paper on the Information Habits of Col-lege Students: How Academic Librarians Can Influence Students' Web-Based Information Choices" (June 2002); Deborah J. Grimes and Carl H. Boening, "Worries with the Web: A Look at Student Use of Web Resources," *College and Research Libraries* 62 (January 2001): 11–23; Shippensburg University, Ezra Lehman Memorial Library, "Internet Use Survey—Analysis," September 26, 2000, www.ship.edu/~bhl/survey; Bradley P. Tolppanen, "A Survey of World Wide Web Use by Freshman English Students: Results and Implications for Bibliographic Instruction," *Internet Reference Services Quarterly* 4 (1999): 43–53; and John Lubans, "How First-Year Students Use and Regard Internet Resources" (1998), www.lubans.org/docs/1styear/firstyear.html.

5. Columbia University, "Electronic Publishing Initiative (EPIC)" (2004), www.epic.columbia.edu/eval/eval04frame.html.

6. John Lubans, "How First-Year Students Use and Regard Internet Resources," December 16, 2004, www.lubans.org/docs/1styear/firstyear.html of Web Resources," *College and Research Libraries* 62 (January 2001): 11–23.

7. Scholz-Crane, "Evaluating the Future: A Preliminary Study of the Process of How Undergraduate Students Evaluate Web Sources," *Reference Services Review* 26 (Fall/Winter 1998): 53–60; Deborah J. Grimes and Carl H. Boening, "Worries with the Web: A Look at Student Use of Web Resources," *College and Research Libraries* 62 (January 2001): 11–23; and Marc Meola, "Chucking the Checklist: A Contextual Approach to Teaching Undergraduates Web-Site Evaluation," *Portal: Libraries and the Academe* 4, no. 3 (2004): 331–44.

8. Meola, "Chucking the Checklist."

9. Vinton G. Cerf, www.isoc.org/internet/conduct/truth.shtml.

10. Columbia University, "Electronic Publishing Initiative (EPIC)" (2004), www.epic.columbia.edu/eval/eval04frame.html.

11. D. G. Kehl and Howard Livingston, "Doublespeak Detection for the Classroom," *English Journal* 88 (July 1999): 79. For further discussion, see Kehl's "The Two Most Powerful Weapons against Doublespeak," *English Journal* 77 (March 1988): 57–65.

12. The *Oxford Dictionary of Quotations*, 5th ed., s.v. "Alexandre Dumas ('Dumas fils') 1824–1895."

13. Don Fallis, "On Verifying the Accuracy of Information: Philosophical Perspectives," *Library Trends* 53, no. 3 (Winter 2004): 470.

14. Ann Coulter, *Slander: Liberal Lies about the American Right* (New York: Three Rivers, 2002), 251.

15. Laurie Mylroie, *The War against America: Saddam Hussein and the World Trade Center Attacks: A Study of Revenge,* 2nd ed. (New York: Regan, 2001), 2.

16. Carl M. Cannon, "The Real Computer Virus," *American Journalism Review* (April 2001): 29.

17. Cannon, "Real Computer Virus," 30.

18. Anthony G. Crocco, et al., "Analysis of Cases of Harm Associated with Use of Health Information on the Internet," *JAMA: Journal of the American Medical Association* 287, no.21 (June 5, 2002): 2869.

19. Paul S. Piper, "Better Read That Again: Web Hoaxes and Misinformation." *Searcher* (September 2000), 41.

20. Robert Ian Scott, "Politics, Advertising, and Excuses: Why Do We Lie?" *ETC: Review of General Semantics* 61 no. 2 (July 2004): 189.

21. Penny Bender and Susan Revah, "Jumping to Conclusions in Oklahoma City?" *American Journalism Review* (June 1995) 11–12; and Said Deep, "Rush to Judgment," *Quill* (July/August 1995): 18.

22. Sonia Bodi, "Scholarship or Propaganda: How Can Librarians Help Undergraduates Tell the Difference?" *Journal of Academic Librarianship* 21, no. 1 (January 1995): 22.

23. Patrick Nuttgens, *What Should We Teach and How Should We Teach It?: Aims and Purpose of Higher Education* (Hants, England: Wildwood House, 1988): 154.

24. The list is based on the work of David Martinson, "Just Propaganda? More Than a Simple Semantics Question for Social Studies Teachers—and Their Students," *Contemporary Education* 71, no. 3 (2000): 49–52; J. C. Merrill, *Journalism Ethics: Philosophical Foundations for News Media* (New York: St. Martin's, 1997); J. A. Jaksa and M. S. Pritchard, *Communications Ethics: Methods of Analysis* (Belmont, CA: Wadsworth, 1994); and Scott, "Politics, Advertising, and Excuses."

25. Garth Jowett and Victoria O'Donnell, *Propaganda and Persuasion* (Newbury Park: Sage, 1999).

26. Green, "Playing Dirty," 321.

27. Wolf Blitzer, "Vice President Gore Calls for Continuation of Clinton Administration Policies: President Promises More Aid to Central America," transcript CNN Late Edition with Wolf Blitzer, March 9, 1999.

28. For more ideas, see Marsha Ann Tate, "Looking for Laura Secord on the Web: Using a Famous Figure from the War of 1812 as a Model for Evaluating Historical Web Sites," *History Teacher* 38, no.2 (2005): 225–40.

29. See related articles on the evaluation of medical websites: "Internet Information on Hip Replacement Surgery Not Always Accurate," *Health News* 11 no. 7 (2005): 5; "Web Site Revised after Bias Complaints," *AIDS Patient Care STDS* 19, no. 7 (2005): 472; C. Escoffery, "Internet Use for Health Information among College Students," *Journal of American College Health* 53, no. 4 (2005): 183–88; I. Hajjar, "Quality of Internet Geriatric Health Information: The Geriatric Web Project," *Journal of the American Geriatrics Society* 53, no. 5 (2005): 885–90; Mark L. Norris, "Ana and the Internet: A Review of Pro-Anorexia Web Sites," *International Journal of Eating Disorders* 39, no.6 (2006): 443–47; and U. Shaikh, "Extent, Accuracy and Credibility of Breastfeeding Information on the Internet," *Journal of Human Lactation* 21, no. 2 (2005): 175–83.

30. For text of the study, see K. J. Jorgensen and P. C. Gotzshe, *British Medical Journal* 328, no. 7432 (January 17, 2004), 148+, (bmj.bmjjournals. com/cgi/content/full/328/7432/148).

BIBLIOGRAPHY

INTRODUCTION

Buschman, John, and Dorothy A. Warner. "Researching and Shaping Information Literacy Initiatives in Relation to the Web: Some Framework Problems and Needs." *Journal of Academic Librarianship* 31, no. 1 (January 2005): 12–18.

Ford, J. E., ed. *Teaching the Research Paper from Theory to Practice, from Research to Writing.* Metuchen, NJ: Scarecrow, 1995.

Gedeon, Randle. "Enhancing a Large Lecture with Active Learning." *Research Strategies* 15, no. 4:301–9.

Goad, Tom. *Information Literacy and Performance.* Westport, CT: Quorum, 2002.

Gradowski, Gail, Loanne Snaveley, and Paula Dempsey, eds. *Designs for Active Learning: A Sourcebook of Classroom Strategies for Information Education.* Chicago: Association of College and Research Libraries, 1998.

Iannuzzi, Patricia. *Teaching Information Literacy Skills.* Boston: Allyn and Bacon, 1999.

Jacobson, Trudi. *Teaching the New Library to Today's Users.* New York: Neal-Schuman, 2000.

Jacobson, Trudi, and Lijuan Xu. *Motivating Students in Information Literacy Classes.* New York: Neal-Schuman, 2004.

Kuhlthau, Carol C. *Teaching the Library Research Process.* Metuchen, NJ: Scarecrow, 1994.

————. *Seeking Meaning: A Process to Library Information Services.* Westport, CT: Libraries Unlimited, 2004.

————. "Role of Experience in the Information Search Process of an Early Career Information Worker: Perceptions of Uncertainty, Complexity, Construction, and Sources." *Journal of the American Society for Information Science (JASIS)* 50, no. 5 (1999): 399–412.

McFadden, T. G. "Computer-Based Instruction in Libraries and Library Education." *Library Trends* [special issue] 50, no. 1 (2001): 1–162.

Pawley, Christine. "Information Literacy: A Contradictory Coupling." *Library Quarterly* 73, no. 4 (2003): 422–52.

Pelikan, Michael. "Problem-Based Learning in the Library: Evolving a Realistic Approach." *Portal: Libraries and the Academy* 4, no. 4 (2004): 509–20.

Perry, Edwin. "The Historical Development of Computer-Assisted Literature Searching and Its Effects on Librarians and Clients." *Library Software Review* 11, no. 2 (1992): 18–24.

Rockman, Ilene. *Integrating Information Literacy into the Higher Education Curriculum: Practical Models for Transformation.* San Francisco: Jossey-Bass, 2004.

Ruggiero, Vincent Ryan. *Changing Attitudes: A Strategy for Motivating Students to Learn.* Needham Heights, MA: Allyn and Bacon, 1998.

Simmons, Michelle Holschuh. "Librarians as Disciplinary Discourse Mediators: Using Genre Theory to Move toward Critical Information Literacy." *Portal: Libraries and the Academy* 5, no. 3 (2005): 297–311.

Snavely, Loanne. "Making Problem-Based Learning Work: Institutional Challenges." *Portal: Libraries and the Academy* 4, no. 4 (2004): 521–31.

Tulgan, Bruce. *Managing Generation X: How to Bring Out the Best in Young Talent.* New York: W. W. Norton, 2000.

Webb, Jo, and Chris Powis. *Teaching Information Skills: Theory and Practice.* London: Facet Publishing, 2004.

Weiler, Angela. "Information Seeking Behavior in Generation Y Students." *Journal of Academic Librarianship* 31, no. 1 (January 2005): 46–53.

CHAPTER I

Badke, William B. *Research Strategies: Finding Your Way through the Information Fog.* 2nd ed. New York: iUniverse, 2004.

Ballenger, Bruce. *The Curious Researcher: A Guide to Writing Research Papers.* 3rd ed. Boston: Allyn and Bacon, 2001.

Berke, Jacqueline, and Randal Woodland. *Twenty Questions for the Writer: A Rhetoric with Readings.* 6th ed. Fort Worth: Harcourt Brace, 1995.

Blazek, Ron. *A Selective Guide to Information Sources*. Englewood, CO: Libraries Unlimited, 2000.

Burke, Kenneth. *A Grammar of Motives*. New York: Prentice-Hall, 1945.

Cryer, Pat. *The Research Student's Guide to Success*. 2nd ed. Philadelphia, PA: Open University Press, 2000.

D'Aniello, Charles A., ed. *Teaching Bibliographic Skills in History: A Sourcebook for Historians and Librarians*. Westport, CT: Greenwood, 1993.

Diaz, Karen, and Nancy O'Hanlon. *IssueWeb: A Guide and Sourcebook for Researching Controversial Issues on the Web*. Westport, CT: Libraries Unlimited: 2004.

Edgington, William D. "Solving Problems with Twenty Questions." *Social Education* 65 (2001): 379–82.

Ford, James. *Teaching the Research Paper: From Theory to Practice, From Research to Writing*. Metuchen, NJ: Scarecrow, 1995.

Hairston, Maxine, and John J. Ruszkiewice. *The Scott Foresman Handbook for Writers*. 3rd ed. New York: HarperCollins, 1993.

Hult, Christine A. *The New Century Handbook*. 3rd ed. New York: Longman, 2005.

Johnson, William J., et al. *The Criminal Justice Student Writer's Manual*. 2nd ed. Upper Saddle River, NJ: Prentice Hall, 2002.

Lane, Nancy, Margaret Chisholm, and Carolyn Mateer. *Techniques for Student Research: A Comprehensive Guide to Using the Library*. New York: Neal-Schuman, 2000.

Maner, Martin. *The Research Process: A Complete Guide and Reference for Writers*. 2nd ed. Mountain View, CA: Mayfield, 2000.

Mann, Thomas. *The Oxford Guide to Library Research*. 3rd ed. New York: Oxford University Press, 2005.

Mitchell, Mark L. *Writing for Psychology: A Guide for Students*. Belmont, CA: Wadsworth/Thomson, 2004.

Northey, Margot, and David B. Knight. *Making Sense: A Student's Guide to Research and Writing: Geography and Environmental Sciences*. 2nd ed. Don Mills, Ontario: Oxford University Press, 2001.

Osborn, Alex F. *Applied Imagination; Principles and Procedures of Creative Problem Solving*. New York: Scribner, 1961.

Pechenik, Jan A. *A Short Guide to Writing about Biology*. 5th ed. New York: Pearson Longman, 2004.

Peterson, Rai. *Real World Research: Sources and Strategies for Composition*. Boston: Houghton Mifflin, 2000.

Quaratiello, Arlene Rodda. *The College Student's Research Companion*. 3rd ed. New York: Neal-Schuman, 2003.

Rosnow, Ralph L. *Writing Papers in Psychology*. 6th ed. Belmont, CA.: Thomson/Wadsworth, 2003.

Ryan, Jenny. *Research Projects: An Information Literacy Planner for Students*. Chicago: American Library Association, 2001.

Schrecengost, Maity. *Teacher's Guide to Researching Issues*. Fort Atkinson, WI: Upstart, 2002.

Smith, Trixie G. "Keeping Track: Librarians, Composition Instructors, and Student Writers Use the Research Journal." *Research Strategies* 18 (2001): 21–28.

Sociology Writing Group. *A Guide to Writing Sociology Papers*. 5th ed. New York: Worth, 2001.

Veit, Richard. *Research: The Student's Guide to Writing Research Papers*. 4th ed. New York: Pearson and Longman, 2004.

Weidenborner, Stephen. *Writing Research Papers: A Guide to the Process*. 6th ed. Boston: St. Martin's, 2001.

Winkler, Anthony C. *Writing the Research Paper: A Handbook*. 6th ed. Austin, TX: Thomson and Heinle, 2003.

CHAPTER 2

Skwire, David. *Writing with a Thesis*. 5th Ed. New York: Holt, 1990.

CHAPTER 3

Allen, Bryce L. "Boolean Browsing in an Information System: An Experimental Test." *Information Technology and Libraries* 201 (2001).

Alter, Catherine. "Logic Modeling: A Tool for Teaching Critical Thinking in Social Work Practice." *Journal of Social Work Education* 33 (1997): 85–100.

Bronander, Kirk A., et al., "Boolean Search Experience and Abilities of Medical Students and Practicing Physicians." *Teaching and Learning Medicine* 14, no.3 (2004): 284–89.

Cody, Dean E. "Critical Thoughts on Critical Thinking." *Journal of Academic Librarianship* 32 (2006): 403–7.

Houghton, Janaye M., and Robert M. Houghton. *Decision Points: Boolean Logic for Computer Users and Beginning Online Searchers*. Englewood, CO: Libraries Unlimited, 1999.

McKibben, K. Ann, Nancy L. Wilcznnski, and R. Brian Haynes. "Developing Optimal Search Strategies for Retrieving Qualitative Studies from PsycInfo." *Evaluation and the Health Professions* 29 no.4 (2006):440–54.

Nahl, Diane, and Violet H. Harada. "Composing Boolean Search Statements: Self Confidence, Concept Analysis, Search Logic, and Errors." *School Library Media Quarterly* 24 (1996): 199–207.

Paris, Lee Anne H., and Helen R. Tibbo. "Freestyle vs. Boolean: A Comparison of Partial and Exact Match Retrieval Systems." *Information Processing and Management* 34 (1998): 284–98.

Shinichi, Monoi, Nancy O'Hanlon, and Karen Diaz. "Online Searching Skills: Development of an Inventory to Assess Self-Efficacy." *Journal of Academic Librarianship* 31, no. 2 (March 2005): 98–105.

Sood, Amit, Patricia J. Erwin, and Jon O. Ebbert. "Using Advanced Search Tools on PubMed for Citation Retrieval." *Mayo Clinic Proceedings* 79, no. 10 (2004): 1295–1300.

Wilcznski, Nancy L., et al. "Optimal Search Strategies for Detecting Health Services Research Studies in Medline." *CMAJ: Canadian Medical Association Journal* 171, no. 10 (2004): 1179–85.

CHAPTER 4

Banta, Martha. "Periodicals Back (Advertisers) to Front (Editors)." In *Reciprocal Influences: Literary Production, Distribution, and Consumption in America.*, 173–98. Columbus: Ohio State University Press.

Carr, Patrick. "Beyond the Monograph: The Uses of Journal Literature by Humanities Scholars at Mississippi State University." *Collection Management* 30, no. 2 (2006): 3–17.

Dain, Phyllis, and John Y. Cole. *Libraries and Scholarly Communication in the United States: The Historical Dimension.* New York: Greenwood, 1990.

Henson, Kenneth. "Writing for Professional Journals: Paradoxes and Promises." *Phi Delta Kappan* 82, no. 10 (June 2001): 765–68.

Hernon, Peter, and Candy Schwartz. "Peer Review Revisited: An Editorial." *Library and Information Science Research* 28 (2006): 1–3.

Hogshire, Jim. *Grossed Out Surgeon Vomits inside Patient: An Insider's Looks at Supermarket Tabloids.* Venice, CA: Feral House, 1997.

Johnson, Sammye, and Patricia Prijatel. *The Magazine: From Cover to Cover.* Chicago: NTC, 1999.

Kling, Rob, and Ewa Callahan. "Electronic Journals, the Internet, Scholarly Communication." *Annual Review of Information Science and Technology* 37 (January 2004).

Knight, Nan. "The Peer Review Process: Where the Jury Is on Your Side." *Chemical and Engineering News* (2003).

Krause, Steven D. "Blogs as a Tool for Teaching." *Chronicle of Higher Education* (June 24, 2005): B33.

Miller, Joann, and Robert Perrucci. "Back Stage at Social Problems: An Analysis of the Editorial Decision Process, 1993–1996." *Social Problems* 48, no. 1 (February 2001): 93–110.

Sparks, Colin, and John Tulloch, eds. *Tabloid Tales: Global Debates over Media Standards.* New York: Rowman & Littlefield, 2000.

CHAPTER 5

Bower, Rick J. "The Development of an Online Library Instruction Tutorial at Pellissippi State Technical Community College." *Community and Junior College Libraries* 9, no. 2 (2000): 15–25.

Dewald, Nancy H. "What Do They Tell Their Students? Business Faculty Acceptance of the Web and Library Databases for Student Research." *Journal of Academic Librarianship* 31, no. 3 (2005): 209–16.

Fagan, Jody Condit. "Usability Testing of a Large, Multidisciplinary Library Database: Basic Search and Visual Search." *Information Technology and Libraries* 25, no. 3 (2006): 140–50.

Neuman, Delia. "High School Students' Use of Databases: Results of the National Delphi Study." *Journal of the American Society for Information Science* 46, no. 4 (1995): 284–98.

Perry, Edwin. "The Historical Development of Computer-Assisted Literature Searching and Its Effects on Librarians and Clients." *Library Software Review* 11, no. 2 (1992): 18–24.

Schonfeld, Roger C. *JSTOR: A History.* Princeton, NJ: Princeton University Press, 2003.

CHAPTER 6

Cole, John Young. *For Congress and the Nation: A Chronological History of the Library of Congress through 1975.* Washington, DC: Library of Congress, 1979.

Conaway, James. *America's Library: Story of the Library of Congress 1800–2000.* New Haven, CT: Yale/Library of Congress, 2000.

Highsmith, Carol M. *Library of Congress: America's Memory.* Golden, CO: Fulcrum, 1994.

CHAPTER 7

Connaway, Lynn S. "Online Catalogs from the User's Perspective: The Use of Focus Group Interviews." *College and Research Libraries* 58, no. 5 (September 1997): 403–21.

Dinet, Jérôme, Favart Monik, and Jean-Michell Passerault. "Searching for Information in an Online Public Access Catalogue (OPAC): The Impacts of Information Search Expertise on the Use of Boolean Operators." *Journal of Computer Assisted Learning* 20, no. 5 (October 2004): 338–45.

Fischer, Karen S. "Critical Views of *LCSH*, 1990–2001: The Third Bibliographic Essay." *Cataloging and Classification Quarterly* 41, no. 1 (2005): 63–109.

Graham, Rumi Y. "Subject No-Hits Searches in Academic Library Online Catalog: An Exploration of Two Potential Ameliorations." *College and Research Libraries* 65, no. 1 (January 2004): 36–57.

Hildreth, Charles R. "The Use and Understanding of Keyword Searching in an University Online Catalog." *Information Technology and Libraries*. 16, no. 2 (June 1997): 52–54.

Library of Congress and Karen Calhoun. *The Changing Nature of the Catalog and Its Integration with Other Discovery Tools*: Final Report. Library of Congress (March 17, 2006), www.loc.gov/catdir/calhoun-report-final.pdf.

Novotny, Eric. "I Don't Think I Click: A Protocol Analysis Study of Use of a Library Online Catalog in the Internet Age." *College and Research Libraries* 65, no. 6 (2004): 525–37.

Stone, Alva T., ed. *The LCSH Century: One Hundred Years with the Library of Congress Subject Headings*. New York: Haworth Information, 2000.

Yu, Holly, and Margo Young. "The Impact of Web Search Engines on Subject Searching in OPAC." *Information Technology and Libraries* 23, no. 4 (December 2004): 168–81.

CHAPTER 8

Drewry, John. *Writing Book Reviews*. Boston: The Writer, 1974.

Galvan, Jose L. *Writing Literature Reviews: A Guide for Students of the Social and Behavioral Sciences*. Glendale, CA: Pyrczak, 2004.

Hayden, John O. *The Romantic Reviewers, 1802–1824*. Chicago: University of Chicago, 1968.

Kamerman, Sylvia E., ed. *Book Reviewing: A Guide to Writing Book Reviews for Newspapers, Magazines, Radio, and Television by Leading Book Editors, Critics, and Reviewers*. Boston: The Writer, 1978.

Lindholm-Romantschuk, Ylva. *Scholarly Book Reviewing in Social Sciences and Humanities: The Flow of Ideas within and among Disciplines.* Westport, CT: Greenwood, 1998.

Literary Reviewing. Charlottesville: University Press of Virginia, 1987.

Walford, A. J., ed. *Reviews and Reviewing: A Guide.* Phoenix, AZ: Oryx, 1986.

CHAPTER 9

Ashmore, Beth, and Jill E. Grogg. "Google and OCLC Open Libraries on the Open Web." *Searcher* 14 (2006): 44–52.

Bar-Ilan, Judit. "The Use of Web Search Engines in Information Science Research." *Annual Review of Information Science and Technology* 38 (2004): 231–88.

Battelle, John. *The Search: How Google and Its Rivals Rewrote the Rules of Business and Transformed Our Culture.* New York: Portfolio, 2005.

Berkman, Robert. *The Skeptical Business Searcher: The Information Advisor's Guide to Evaluating Web Data, Sites, and Sources.* Medford, NJ: Information Today, 2004.

Bishop, Ann Peterson, Nancy A. Van House, and Barbara P. Buttenfield, eds. *Digital Library Use: Social Practice in Design and Evaluation.* Cambridge, MA: MIT, 2003.

Browner, Stephanie, Stephen Pulsford, and Richard Sears. *Literature and the Internet.* New York: Garland, 2000.

Block, Marylaine, ed. *The Quintessential Searcher: The Wit and Wisdom of Barbara Quint.* Medford, NJ: Information Today, 2001.

———. "My Rules of Information." *Searcher* 10, no.1 (2002).

Bradley, Phil. *The Advanced Internet Searcher's Handbook.* 3rd ed. London: Facet, 2004.

Buschman, John, and Dorothy A Warner. "Researching and Shaping Information Literacy Initiatives in Relation to the Web: Some Framework Problems and Needs." *Journal of Academic Librarianship* 31, no. 1 (2005): 12–18.

Dornfest, Rael, Paul Bausch, and Tara Calishain. *Google Hacks: Tips and Tools for Finding and Using the World's Information.* 3rd ed. Farnham: O'Reilly Media, 2006.

Clyde, Laura A. *Weblogs and Libraries.* Oxford: Chandos, 2004.

Colaric, Susan M. "Instruction for Web Searching: An Empirical Study." *College and Research Libraries* 64, no.2 (March 2003): 111–22.

Cusumano, Michael. "Google: What It Is and What It Is Not." *Communications of the ACM* 48, no. 2 (2005): 15–17.

Devine, Jane, and Francine Egger-Sider. "Beyond Google: The Invisible Web in the Academic Library." *Journal of Academic Librarianship* 30, no. 4 (July 2004): 265–71.

Doule, Carol, Don Lubach, and Janet Martorana. "Solving the Job Puzzle: A Workshop on Using the Web to Find Career Resources." *Research Strategies* (1997): 100–105.

Ellis, David, and Hanna Oldman. "The English Literature Researcher in the Age of the Internet." *Journal of Information Science* 31, no. 1 (2005): 29–37.

Fox, Steve, et al. "Evaluating Implicit Measures to Improve Web Search." *ACM Transactions on Information Systems* 23, no. 2 (2005): 147.

Heikki, Topi, and Wendy Lucas. "Searching the Web: Operator Assistance Required." *Information Processing and Management* 41, no. 2 (March 2005): 383–403.

Ihadjadene, Madjid, Stephanne Chaudiron, and Daniel Martins. "The Effect of Individual Differences on Searching the Web." Proceedings of the ASIST annual meeting, 2003.

Kay, Heidi, and Karen Delvecchio. *The World at Your Fingertips: Learning Research and Internet Skills.* Fort Atkinson, WI: Highsmith, 2002.

King, Valery, and Diane Zabel. "Music Research and Reference on the Internet. Source." *Reference and User Services Quarterly* 44, no. 2 (Winter 2004): 111–15.

Lackie, Robert J. "The Evolving 'Invisible Web': Tried-and-True Methods and New Developments for Locating the Web's Hidden Content." *College and Undergraduate Libraries* 10, no. 2 (2003): 65–71.

Lazonder, A. W. "Do Two Heads Search Better Than One? Effects of Student Collaboration on Web Search Behavior and Search Outcomes." *British Journal of Educational Technology* 36, no. 3 (2005): 465–75.

Lee, Y. J. "Concept Mapping Your Web Searches: A Design Rationale and Web-Enabled Application." *Journal of Computer-Assisted Learning* 20, no. 2 (2004): 103–13.

Milstein, Sarah, and Rael Dornfest. *Google: The Missing Manual.* Sebastopol, CA: O'Reilly, 2004.

Muller, Jeanne Froidevaux. *A Librarian's Guide to the Internet: Searching and Evaluating.* Oxford, UK: Chandos, 2004.

Niehuas, Chris, et al. "The Depth and Breadth of Google Scholar: An Empirical Study." *Portal: Libraries and the Academy* 6, no. 2 (2006): 127–41.

Notess, Gress. "Web Searching Strategies." (February 2004) notess.com/speak/talks/india/04advanced.pps#l.

Rogers, Donna, and Karen Swan. "Self-Regulated Learning and Internet Searching." *Teachers College Record* 106, no. 9 (2004): 1804–24.

Sherman, Chris. *Google Power: Unleash the Full Potential of Google.* New York: McGraw Hill/Osborne Media, 2005.

Stacey, Alison, and Adrian Stacey. *Effective Information Retrieval from the Internet: An Advanced User's Guide.* Oxford, UK: Chandos, 2004.

Tankard, James W., Jr., and Cindy Royal. "What's on the Web—and What's Not." *Social Science Computer Review* 23, no. 3 (2005): 360.

Thompson, Christen. "Information Illiterate or Lazy: How College Students Use the Web for Research." *Portal: Libraries and the Academy* 3, no. 2 (2003): 259–68.

Tillotson, Joy. "A Portrait of the Audience for Instruction in Web Searching: Results of a Survey Conducted at Two Canadian Universities." *Canadian Journal of Information and Library Science* 27 (March 2002): 3–28.

Vise, David A. *The Google Story.* New York: Bantam Dell, 2005.

Weideman, Melius, and Corrie Strümpfer. "The Effect of Search Engine Keyword Choice and Demographic Features on Internet Searching Success." *Information Technology and Libraries* 23, no. 2 (2004): 58+.

Weiler, A. "Two-Year College Freshmen and the Internet: Do They Really 'Know All That Stuff?'" *Libraries and the Academy* 1, no.2 (2001).

Yu, Holly, and Margo Young. "The Impact of Web Search Engines on Subject Searching in OPAC." *Information Technology and Libraries* 23, no. 4 (2004): 168–80.

Yu-Mei Wang, and Marge Artero. "Caught in the Web: University Student Use of Web Resources." *Educational Media International* 42, no. 1 (March 2005): 71–82.

CHAPTER 10

Burbules, N. C. "Paradoxes of the Web: The Ethical Dimensions of Credibility." *Library Trends* 49, no. 3 (2001): 441–53.

Chen, Hsinchun, Ann M Lally, Bin Zhu, and Michael Chau. "Helpful Med: Intelligent Searching for Medical Information over the Internet." *Journal of the American Society for Information Science and Technology* 54, no. 7 (2003): 683–94.

Colaric, Susan M. "Instruction for Web Searching: An Empirical Study." *College and Research Libraries* 64, no. 2 (March 2003): 111–22.

Craigie, M., B. Loader, R. Burrows, and S. Muncer. "Reliability of Health Information on the Internet: An Examination of Experts' Ratings." *Journal of Medical Internet Research* 4, no. 1 (2002): E2.

Dewald, Nancy H. "What Do They Tell Their Students? Business Faculty Acceptance of the Web and Library Databases for Student Research." *Jour-*

nal of Academic Librarianship 31, no. 3 (2005): 209–15.

Fritch, John W. "Evaluating Internet Resources: Identity, Affiliation, and Cognitive Authority in a Networked World." *Journal of the American Society for Information Science and Technology* 52, no. 6 (2001): 499–507.

———." Heuristics, Tools, and Systems for Evaluating Internet Information: Helping Users Assess a Tangled Web." *Online Information Review* 27, no. 5 (2003): 321–27.

Gillen, Christopher M., Bethany R. Lye, and Jasmine Vaughan. "An Online Tutorial for Helping Non-science Majors Read Primary Research Literature in Biology." *Advances in Physiology Education* 28, no. 4 (2004): 9.

Graham, Leah, and Panagiotis Takis Metaxas. "Of Course It's True; I Saw It on the Internet!" Critical Thinking in the Internet Era." *Communications of the ACM* 46, no. 5 (2003): 71–79.

Jowett, Garth S., and Victoria O'Donnell. *Propaganda and Persuasion.* 2nd ed. Newberry Park, CA: Sage, 1992.

Liu, Ziming. "Perceptions of Credibility of Scholarly Information on the Web." *Information Processing and Management* 40 (2004): 1027–38.

Meola, Marc. "Chucking the Checklist: A Contextual Approach to Teaching Undergraduates Web-Site Evaluation." *Portal: Libraries and the Academy* 4, no. 3 (July 2004): 331–44.

Olson, John A. "How to Encourage Students in a Library Instruction Session to Use Critical and Creative Thinking Skills: A Pilot Study." *Research Strategies* 16, no. 4 (2000): 309–14.

Scott, Robert Ian. "Politics, Advertising, and Excuses: Why Do We Lie?" *ETC: Review of General Semantics* 61, no. 2 (July 2004): 187–95.

Simmons, Michelle Holschuh. "Librarians as Disciplinary Discourse Mediators: Using Genre Theory to Move toward Critical Information Literacy." *Portal: Libraries and the Academy* 5, no. 3 (2005): 297–311.

Stapleton, Paul. "Evaluating Web-Sources: Internet Literacy and L2 Academic Writing." *ELT Journal* 59, no. 2 (2005): 135–43.

Warnick, Barbara. "Online Ethos: Source Credibility in an "Authorless" Environment." *American Behavioral Scientist* 48, no. 2 (2004): 256+.

Weimann, Gabriel. "Virtual Disputes: The Use of the Internet for Terrorist Debates." *Studies in Conflict and Terrorism* 29, no. 7 (2006): 623–39.

Yu-Mei Wang, and Marge Artero. "Caught in the Web: University Student Use of Web Resources." *Educational Media International* 42, no. 1 (2005): 71–82.

INDEX

ABOUT THE AUTHOR

Christy Gavin received her master of library science degree from the University of Southern California. In 1977, she joined the library staff at the California State University in Bakersfield and assumed her current position of coordinator of instructional services in 1987. She teaches courses in information literacy and methods of literary scholarship and is also responsible for the bibliographical areas of anthropology, archaeology, art, English literature, sociology, social work, and theater.

.